Mindfulness Eating

Simple Mindfulness Practices To Nurture A Healthy EATING TO CREATE A HEALING Relationship With Food To End Overeating, Satisfy Your Hunger

By G.S. Hayashi

Table of Contents

Introduction

To start, it involves tuning in with your natural hunger cues. That is, knowing if your body really needs food. According to one study, a stressed brain activates the same mechanisms as a hungry one, so meals are then sought that meet our needs as quickly as possible (those rich in salt or sugar). The problem is that we are not starving, but nervous, anxious or simply bored.

In addition, it about knows when we have had enough, even before our body warns us that we are already satiated (the brain can take up to 20 minutes to let us know that we do not need to continue eating). Therefore, it means knowing how much we need to eat according to the occasion: reduce our rations if we are going to play sports, allow ourselves a little more margin in celebrations and events.

It also means really savoring the food. Eat quietly, chewing, not swallowing. Enjoying the flavors, smells and textures. We are not talking about a diet based on prohibitions. Applying mindfulness to food involves choosing wisely for both health and satisfaction. That is, accept that there are certain products that make you feel good or you like them more than others, and be able to take them without feeling guilty. It is simply about learning to compensate for these little whims, which may not be too 'recommendable', with other healthier choices. So nothing to forget about chocolate, mindfulness has to enjoy it even more.

Conscious feeding is very pleasant. We sit beautifully. We look at the people around us. We look at the food on the plates. This is a profound practice.

Thich Nhat Hanh

The origin of mindful eating

One of the pioneers in this field is the psychologist Jean Kristeller, who treated young university students with obesity problems who ate large amounts of food compulsively (what is known as "binge eating" or binge eating). Kristeller thought that his students had a dysfunctional relationship with food, and that their problem could not be solved simply with a diet. These young people needed to listen to their own bodies to know when they were full and should stop.

When he learned about Jon Kabat-Zinn's work and his MBSR (Mindfulness Based Stress Reduction) method, it came to light. Together with a PhD student, she developed a program called MB-EAT (Mindfulness Based Eating Awareness Training), with which she intended to teach people how to taste their food, recognize their hunger levels and accept their eating preferences.

One of the exercises was to eat a few raisins, savoring them calmly, to demonstrate how this had the same effect as taking an entire package quickly and without paying close attention. Obviously, it seems simple with raisins. The goal is that we be able to apply this same premise to more tempting foods, such as cakes, chocolate or hot dogs.

Kristeller had noticed how most obese people who want to lose weight develop a pattern based on controlling their diet by avoiding certain foods and putting on limitations, believing that everything consists of having willpower. That is why, when something goes wrong and they exceed the limits, they feel that they have spoiled everything and they end up giving up. This is something that can be avoided with mindful eating. There is never a point of no return; you can always eat again with full attention, even if at some point you eat unconsciously or excessively.

The results guarantee it

The MB-EAT program was tested by Kristeller in a first study with a group of 18 compulsive eaters that had no previous experience with meditation. The program consisted of seven sessions, in which they were taught to meditate and practiced various exercises to eat consciously, which were increasing their difficulty when performed with more tempting foods: from raisins to chocolate snacks.

After the program, binge eating had decreased from an average of 4 to 1.5 per week, and only four of the participants remained within the parameters of eating disorder. In addition, women not only reduced their meals, but also demonstrated that they had acquired a better relationship with food and decreased their levels of depression and anxiety. The results were better the more the meditation practices had been followed.

In the second study, which was carried out together with Ruth Quillian-Wolever, from Duke University, the program was tested in a group of obese compulsive eaters, comparing them with two control groups, one of which followed another educational program. Both the MB-EAT group and the other program reduced their binge-eating, but those in the MB-EAT showed signs of having achieved better self-regulation and balance in their meals.

It has been clarified that the practice of mindfulness increases the size and activity of the prefrontal cortex, the area of the brain connected to decision making and long-term plans. Although it has not been proven what happens in the brain when people practice mindful eating, it would make sense to follow the hypothesis that these same areas are reinforced, making it easier for people to cognitively process their desire to eat, rather than feeling victims of emotions that often lead to it.

Start applying mindful eating

The best way to check if mindful eating works is to try it yourself. To begin, it is enough to follow these simple steps that will help you in your purpose of eating consciously. You can read them, watch the video, or do both.

1. Eat slowly

To listen to your body and know how much you should eat, there is nothing better than tranquility. Eat calmly, spending about 20 minutes on a standard size menu.

2. Take 5 minutes to reflect on your food

Think about the whole process before the food has reached your plate. The cultivation, collection and transport. The preparation, cooking and presentation. This will help you focus your mind on eating.

3. Chew well

Take small bites and chew them about 25 or 30 times. Many times we fall into the trap of 'swallowing' our food, but it is necessary to chew it and taste it correctly.

4. Use your non-dominant hand

At first it can be difficult to eat with the necessary calm. To make sure you don't increase your speed without realizing it, you can eat with your non-dominant hand or with chopsticks. By not having practice, your intake rate will be reduced.

5. Avoid distractions

Forget mobile and television. They get us to eat mechanically and not realize if we have eaten enough. Our goal is not to empty the plate, but to satiate ourselves, so we have to focus on our body, not on external elements.

6. Protect yourself from temptation

Although the goal is to learn to eat out of necessity and consciously, temptations exist and, especially at the beginning, are difficult to avoid. Many times we eat because we have food within our reach. As a trick: hide everything you know you don't need and leave healthy options within your reach. If you really fancy a sweet or savory snack, you will look for it (and nothing happens), but you will make sure not to eat it just because you have it within reach.

7. Ask your body

Every time you go straight to the fridge or pantry, ask yourself. "I'm really hungry?" Boredom, stress or, simply, seeing that another is eating are reasons that make us travel to the refrigerator in search of something that satisfies us. When this happens, stop to think if really need food or it has been an impulse motivated by another cause. You will see how more than once your stomach replies that it does not need food. And if you need it, of course, go ahead.

Starting to apply mindfulness to your life is not easy, much less if it is to apply it to something as tempting and rich as food. But we are sure that with these little tricks and a little willpower you will get it at the beginning. Once you enter the dynamic, it will leave you alone!

Mindful food - mindfulness exercises for the home

Certainly when you are busy with mindfulness cooking this is a good addition. Because when you cook, you are really busy with what you are doing at that moment, step by step. With mindful food you do this too. You initially consider what you eat and your eating habits. It is therefore also awareness and possibly an eye opener, for example if you want to eat a little healthier, or if you want to lose weight. In this way you learn to eat with attention. This allows you to eat more slowly, enjoy the food in question and listen better to the signals from your body.

Eating is something that many people do on autopilot. You just have to do it every day, the temptations of food around us are huge, and you can easily do food at the same time as all kinds of other activities. Mindful eating is a method in mindfulness to build a different relationship with food. It is not about what you eat, but about becoming aware of how and why you eat. You achieve this by carefully observing all the food experience. Think about:

- Flavors;
- Fragrances;
- Hunger;

- Saturation;
- Thoughts when eating;
- Emotions with food.

Can I eat mindful?

Just like with all previous mindfulness exercises for home, you can't do anything wrong with mindful eating. There are actually no rules, you don't have to achieve anything, and it can't fail. You just have to be aware of what is happening. Even if things don't go 'perfect'. You notice it, learn something from it and continue with it.

Exercises for mindful eating

Now that you know a little about mindful food, I can imagine that you do not yet know how to do this. I also understand that, because I too had no idea about this at the beginning. And this mindfulness exercise also means that you have to start small. Go try it out in small steps and expand it this way. Where you start with a small and short exercise, you can apply this later while eating, for example, your dinner.

Exercise 1: observing food

This exercise is, as it were, the basis of mindful eating: you give full attention to a small piece of food for a few minutes and use all your senses. You will notice in detail what sensation, thought or feeling that produces at that moment. You could keep it as a talk.

You can do the exercise with different types of food. It is interesting to experience the difference with thoughtless food. And to notice how much surprise there can be in the usual snack. The more often you use this way of eating, the better. It goes without saying that it is not realistic to work like this for a whole meal. This would make the food rather annoying, rather than allowing you to enjoy it more. For example, try doing it with every first bite of a meal or once a day with a snack at a quiet moment.

Exercise 2: tasting

Fine tasting is a short exercise that helps you become a gourmet. Do you actually know what you really like? And why? What is the effect of a certain type of food on you? Are the snacks that you are a fan of really so tasty? You can learn to recognize that by systematically and carefully paying attention to food. The result of this exercise is that you can consciously choose what you really want to eat. This exercise often surprises many people. Sometimes you think you know what you like so much, but this exercise turns out to be different. You can do it with one food, but you can also compare multiple types. For example: different flavors of chips, nuts or pieces of bread. Make sure you really observe what you taste and try not to lead you through your thoughts.

Exercise 3: Experiencing food per bite

After the above short exercises apart from your breakfast, lunch or dinner you can apply this exercise at home during dinner for example. Hereby really pay attention to your food.

1. Sit down and switch off TV, smartphone or laptop;
2. Smell the food, taste the food while you chew. Try to distinguish the flavors, experience the structure;
3. Keep your attention when eating. If you stray, you simply get your attention back to the sensation of the food.

This will make your food taste more intense. If you repeat this exercise from time to time and with some regularity, you will even be able to distinguish artificial substances from fair nutrients.

Exercise 4: wait with the next bite

We are soon inclined to push one bite after the other. Don't do this. Taste, chew, experience, swallow and wait for the food to sink down towards your stomach. Then take the next bite.

By eating this way you prevent many problems (abdominal pain, heartburn, farmers, intestinal complaints) and you experience eating much more intensely. It also helps you relax. You can eat really relaxed in this way.

Quiet food ensures that you really take the time to eat. And that's great, because your body needs time to process the incoming food. Only after about twenty minutes do your brains get a signal that food is coming in! So it comes only later that you are full. Because of this we often eat too much, because we eat too fast, we notice it too late. If you eat this way, you can also stop in time because you will experience the full feeling on time.

The Four Pillars Of Mindful Essen

We know that terms like mindfulness or attention are fashion-conscious. But sometimes, some people follow a trend like mindfulness, uncomprehending with real amplitude all the pillars on which it rests. Not just talk about some kind of meditation, a way to combat stress or to implement a relaxation method.

Mindfulness is a window through life so present, close and authentic to see. It forces us to stop progressing in the thicket of the forest to recognize where our roots are and, above all, they feel. Lives now does not mean finding a hole 18-19.30 to meditate peace. It means acquiring a new life plan, a new perspective that is certainly an integral part of food.

Let's see what form the assumptions are attentively eating.

1. That's not just about what you eat, but how you eat

We eat in 20 minutes for anything, go back to work. We fed with stimuli, with the television blaring, with a sandwich and the phone in the other. Even more, sometimes we are more aware that talking to friends or our relatives cooks up in front of us.

You have to change routines as long as we can. To do this, keep these simple tips in mind:

- Reduce the largest number of stimuli noon.
- Prevents the table from having many dishes or many types of food. Redúcete on the essentials: first cup and another then.
- Come in a quiet place.
- When family food makes sure the atmosphere is relaxed.

2. Are you really hungry or want to fill an emotional gap?

Everything we ever did. Get tired home, overwhelmed by anxiety and frustration to saturate our minds. At that moment, really, something sweet or something savory: ice cream, pizza with a lot of cheese, a bowl of chocolate or a few chips...

Surely we are talking about those moments when food becomes an emotional catharsis. This excessive intake, which gradually gets more pounds, can lead to frustration and later to a jail that costs us a lot.

As we beat to mindful food our bodies feed, eat hunger to satisfy, never to emotions.

3. No hurry, food tastes, textures, flavors

Chew slowly the acid explosion of strawberries feeling, crowned by the white yogurt, where bits of nuts and oats hide, a delicious combination where our brain appreciates the presence of glucose, antioxidants, vitamins and fiber...

When was the last moment you ate breakfast in peace? Mindful food invites us to start eating more slowly, chewing lots of every food, every piece of fruit, every plant, every piece of meat ... If you do it quietly, you will be satisfied much sooner and the amount of food will be satisfying Your body will be fair and necessary.

Always remember that most people are advised to eat everything, but in the right amount. Few things are more appropriate to eat 5 times a day in small portions before succumbing to the classic binge eating dinner.

4. Exercise during the day and drink in front of a glass of drinking water

Surely you are also someone who serves the table when often put a glass of water next to the plate. It is not appropriate. Ideally, drink the glass of water 15 minutes before eating. So we prepare our bodies for later feeding and facilitate turning digestion.

Also, we cannot forget something as fundamental as our bodies and minds exercise. In fact, it would be enough to take a day a walk for half an hour. It's a sensational way to work your heart while your mind is released, resting and oxygenating.

The Attentive Eating suggests its "intuitive eater" to start. Before resorting to strict diets, counting calories, or restricting food to fast or to a strategy that threatens our health, is the ideal to listen to your own body and its needs.

Above all, this means knowing how to control emotions appropriately. smart, aware Let's put it into practice and learn to gradually connect with our body a bit more.

Cooking Mindfulness - Mindfulness exercises for the home

Cooking with attention

It is probably very familiar to everyone: a busy day and the thought of having to put the food on the table. You look forward to cooking and you get something easy, or you quickly throw something into different pans, which makes you rush to cook. You can also look at it differently, because you can get a lot of satisfaction from cooking. You do this by cooking with attention, in short mindfulness cooking. Another completely different mindfulness exercise for the home, such as breathing exercises. You are going to apply mindfulness in your daily activities at home, so that you really come to live in the here and now. And that is what you want to achieve.

How can you cook mindfulness?

It may sound silly or too good to be true. How can you cook quietly after a busy day when you are tired? It is really possible. Try it by starting with the following:

- Schedule the actions so that you don't have to rush. You do this by doing everything step by step;

- So do not put the water on when boiling the pasta, but start making the sauce;
- When making the sauce, carefully cut the vegetables with attention and take time for possible mashing and stirring;
- Is the sauce ready? Then turn on the water and sit quietly in between;
- Then cook the pasta and then set the table at ease;
- Afterwards, really enjoy the food. So apply mindful food after mindful cooking.
- When you cook in this way, you will find that you naturally enjoy the food itself more. It will taste better and you will therefore eat less in a hurry.

Deliberately enjoy cooking

With mindfulness cooking it is therefore the intention that you consciously enjoy it. You are really busy here and in the now. So it is not the intention that while cooking you are already thinking about what you will do next, or that you have to hurry up because you want to watch your Netflix series tonight. As already mentioned, you can sit quietly in between when, for example, you boil the water for the pasta. After all, you had already prepared the sauce with attention. In order not to stray away and enjoy the peace and quiet at the moment you rest, you can, for example, apply the mindfulness exercises for home for immediate rest.

With mindfulness cooking, you prepare the food without hurry and especially not with the automatic pilot. Sounds great right?

Cooking recipe for mindfulness

Maybe you want to try mindfulness cooking and are you looking for a recipe. Then certainly not too difficult and start easily. Above I am talking about cooking pasta. That is why I want to give you an easy recipe, so that you can give it a try and you don't have to start immediately. After all, one person can cook better than the other. And some people really don't like cooking. In that case, try to give it a positive twist. You do this by certainly not starting with difficult recipes. Just keep it simple in the beginning so that you are not distracted and can keep your attention. The recipe below is really not difficult.

Tagliatelle with zucchini, salmon and cream cheese

What do you need? Groceries:

Olive oil, 2 tablespoons;

Fresh chives 25 grams;

Dairy spread chives light 200 grams;

Lemon once;

Salmon fillet 300 grams;

Zucchini once;

Tagliatelle 250 grams.

The preparation of the pasta:

Follow the steps below step by step:

1. Start cutting the zucchini;
2. After this you cut the salmon into cubes of 1 cm;
3. Heat the oil inside a non-stick pan and fry the zucchini cubes in 2 minutes;
4. Add the salmon cubes and fry for 1 minute;
5. Then add the cream cheese and turn off the heat. This way the cream cheese can melt smoothly;
6. Finely chop the chives and mix this with the mixture of zucchini, salmon cubes and cream cheese.
7. Now put the water for the pasta on and let it boil;

8. Add the tagliatelle into the boiling water and cook for 10 minutes;
9. Drain the pasta and mix it into the mixture;
10. Season it with lemon juice and salt and pepper;

This is the order to cook mindfulness with this recipe. If you were just cooking this, you would probably start by setting up the water, boiling the pasta and making the mixture in a hurry. That way you are already cooking and your thoughts are spreading in all directions and that is precisely what you do not want. By following the steps above you are really cooking consciously. In the meantime, the water almost runs into your mouth, so that the food will definitely taste good after cooking.

To alternate, you can also make a salad as a side dish with the above recipe. The most convenient is to make this salad for preparing the mixture and pasta. There are of course many types and tastes of salads. Whatever salad you make, with whatever ingredients, make sure you first cut the vegetables carefully, then mix them and then put it in the fridge for a while so that you can serve it with the main course.

Try cooking mindfulness at home on the weekend to get started. You will see that it has a very relaxed effect.

How To Develop Mindful Eating Practice

The transition to the New Year is usually a time when we commit to changing something of ourselves. In these holidays it is easy for our relationship with food to be more critical and conflicting. These are moments of "good" purposes such as "dieting", losing weight or leaving something that causes us suffering.

However, dieting is not one of those good purposes. It cannot be considered a skillful purpose to make war on kilos or take certain foods to jail because they are guilty of our suffering.

We know that diets are not a good way to tackle problems, a path that supposes a restriction of food for our body is a form of violence that does not usually end well. Experience tells us that restrictions stimulate desire, that prohibitions can only be maintained with an effort that generates great resistance. This resistance is directly proportional to all the effort and control that we are accumulating and there comes a time when all that effort made is of such magnitude that that resistance becomes an avalanche of desire that overflows us and leads us to eat compulsively and in greater quantity.

The evidence tells us that treatments for obesity that are based on a restrictive eating plan fail in the long term, have significant negative effects in terms of self-esteem and health. And on the other hand, we also know that dieting is the most important predictor of the appearance of an eating disorder. The earlier the age at which a person begins dieting, the more risk he has of developing an eating disorder.

That is why it is important to focus a change in our relationship with food and reorient our relationship with it from a perspective of compassion, generosity and forgiveness.

Eating mindful is a perspective that allows us to approach difficulties from kindness, acceptance and lack of judgment is a radical change that allows us to open ourselves to new ways of relating to our problems, with food and with life in general.

Eating with mindful attention or mindful eating has been described by Jan Chozen Bays as "... an experience that involves body, mind, heart and spirit to choose, prepare and eat food." It allows us to be curious to investigate our responses to food and food. our inner signals of hunger and satiety, and nurture ourselves by listening to the wisdom of our body. In this way, mindful eating allows us to make choices that promote health and well-being.

From the perspective of mindful eating, the idea of labeling food as “good” or “bad” is abandoned, calories are not counted, diets are not prescribed, and it is not said what “should” or “should not be” eaten or prohibited or restricted foods. Instead, awareness of the internal signs of hunger and satiety is cultivated and the wisdom of our body begins to be rediscovered.

How to create daily practice of mindful eating

Make a commitment and spend a few minutes each day to practice conscious eating. Maybe you can commit to having a bite with mindfulness in one meal a day.

To do this you can follow these steps:

1. Take a piece of a food

It is useful to begin this conscious practice of eating with a small amount of a type of food that is not a trigger for compulsive desire (a food that does not stimulate the desire to overeat.) For example, a simple meal option may be a carrot, one or two grapes or banana slices. As we practice attention we can choose the most difficult foods, such as a thin potato, an ounce of chocolate or cookies.

2. Look at the food

Look at the shape, color or its nuances

3. Touch the food

Look at the texture. Close your eyes to look at it with touch.

4. Smell the food

Aspire its aroma and notice how you respond to the experience

5. Observe your thoughts and emotions

Perhaps anticipatory thoughts arise, It will be very good, with a piece it will not be enough. I hope there is more. ”Or, perhaps a feeling of disappointment arises,“ It's just a grape, not chocolate cake. ” Let thoughts arise and fade away.

6. Savor the food

Put it on your tongue. Note how your tongue and salivary glands respond.

7. Bite the food

Do not take it in a bite. Note the texture and sounds when chewing.

8. Chew the food

When you start chewing, notice the explosion of flavor, acidity, sweetness, or any sensation that arises. Watch as the taste arises and as it begins to fade, there may be a strong desire to want another piece, even while you are still eating this bite.

Try to relax. Stay with what you are actually experiencing, instead of looking for a new flavor shot.

9. Swallow the food

Take some time to observe the sensations of how the mouthful passes from your mouth to the stomach. And how food begins to be absorbed in the stomach. How does your stomach respond to food?

10. Name the food

Yes, say it quietly. Appreciate it and say thank you.

11. Experience the power to decide

By exercising, eat with mindfulness and experience together what we feel in our body and what we experience in our mind. We can discover that we have a choice: we can really taste and experience what we are eating, or we can eat awkwardly and gobble up with hardly any awareness. As we are able to tune into our ability to taste, consciously recognize the value of food, this practice can help us discover what lies behind desire.

12. Take a mindful bite once at each meal

Appreciate your food by providing mindfulness with this simple exercise. Start this exercise every meal over and over again. There is much to observe, flavors to experience, a continuous journey full of hours.

Mindfulness At Lunchtime

By eating this way, one awakens your intuition. That is, the inner wisdom itself.

There is a thought that many people have and it is "all or nothing" . That is, either they live in food restriction or they eat the world. There is no middle. This comes from a clear disconnection with oneself. That is why I am so interested that people learn to eat with full awareness. This means eating with attention to the flavors and the food that one is eating, and feeding with the intention of using the food to enjoy and nourish.

Initially

One comes to the world knowing how to eat intuitively. Babies cry when they are hungry and do not stop until they feel satiated. When they are physically full, they spit whatever food one forces them to eat. Along the way, most unlearn that intuitive feed.

When was the last time they served on a plate what they were going to "chop" to enjoy it, instead of taking it out of the pantry and eating it stopped, and then continue eating other things? Or the last time they tasted every piece of chocolate without biting it right away and finishing it whole in a minute? And the last time they ate a piece of candy or "forbidden food" without guilt?

The idea that one can rely on his body to guide him in making food choices is totally strange. When one develops the practice of eating intuitively, one can set aside the external messages that dictate what, how much and how one should eat, because these messages only increase the desire for restricted food. For example, when one wants cookies, but refrains from a message received that it is not good. So you eat an apple, cheese, jelly, etc., in a short period of time, until you reach what you initially wanted, which are cookies.

YOU CAN BE INTERESTED: Are you an emotional eater? Six tips to stop being

If you have had the habit of thinking about "forbidden foods," allowing yourself to choose any food you want can be scary. At the beginning of practicing eating with intuition it is possible that the same body leans towards this type of food. But when you listen closely to what your body asks, you can realize that the craving for a certain food will decrease by allowing you to eat it. Over time the mental structures will change and the desire for forbidden foods will decrease. You will also lose interest in eating without hunger.

When eating with full awareness one experiences with food, since there are no “forbidden” or “allowed” labels. One can learn which foods satisfy him, give him warmth and nourish him, and which ones cause him discomfort. Thus, each person internalizes how he feels after eating different foods, in different amounts. If one eats beyond the point where one feels satiated, the important thing is to be kind to oneself, since at the beginning of this practice one is in a period of trial and error. By knowing how you want to feel when you finish eating, and by remembering past experiences of eating different foods in different amounts, you develop the ability to choose more balanced meals more easily. If one becomes aware of the discomfort of the moment, one has a better chance of remembering the bodily sensations and emotions that one does not want to repeat.

Benefits of eating with intuition

By learning to eat in this way, one becomes an intuitive person in all aspects of his life. When you take time to listen to your body, you can also learn other needs that are not related to food at all. All people experience hunger for other things that are not food. By being aware, they can do a mental test of whether what is really desired is food or something else. When you realize that you want to eat without physical hunger, you can ask yourself the following questions: Is food what I want or something else? What am i feeling? Boredom, stress, anxiety, loneliness, fear? Do I need creativity, company, movement, time to breathe deeply, spiritual connection, rest? What obstacles are blocking my ability to meet my needs? Will eating satisfy what I need?

By trusting in the most basic and primitive, one can begin to hear oneself at a deeper level. Intuition itself allows everyone to know the reality about who they are, what their purpose is and how they feel in different relationships. Instead of being so worried about what others think they should do, one remains connected with what they know is right for themselves. No matter how difficult the road is. Internal wisdom frees one from ambivalence.

The most important thing is that you learn to be in tune with what you need and with what you can adapt to your lifestyle. An obstacle that keeps people from trusting their intuition is the thought that there is another person responsible for deciding what they need and that there is another expert on their body.

When an intuition approach is adopted, decisions about what, when and how much is eaten, how much to move and when to rest become their own decisions. No rules. Everyone decides what they need. And little by little one feels able to trust his ability to decide what he needs.

Thus one understands that each person is a world and that all people work something different. Caring for health will never be the same for everyone. If you have a complicated relationship with food, doing your best may be allowing yourself to savor a portion of something you usually feel guilty about eating every day. There may also be people who loved to eat candy every day, but by eating with intuition they realize that with a candy a day they can taste it and enjoy it, and they feel good. On the contrary, there may be someone who loves to eat healthy and who does not give pleasure to enjoy a few sweets a week. The gain in health for that person has another meaning. Another example: Exercising can be something totally different for someone who works than for someone who does not, for the time available. Everyone adapts to their circumstances, tuning in and around them.

Anyway, if a person has learned to manage emotions with food and to be on an autopilot in everyday life, it may sound almost impossible to make this change, but the more you practice it, the more awareness you will create and the more tools you will develop for a relationship healthy and balanced with food, with himself and with situations.

Careful eating is a technique that helps you control your eating habits.

It has been shown to increase weight loss, reduce eating disorders and help you feel better.

What is careful eating?

Careful eating is based on the consideration of having a Buddhist concept.

Awareness is a form of meditation that helps you to recognize and deal with your emotions and physical sensations.

It is used for treat various conditions and eating disorders, depression, anxiety, and various food-related behaviors.

Careful eating is about using awareness to achieve a state of full attention through your experiences, desires and physical cues during eating.

Basically, careful eating includes:

- eat slowly and without distractions,
- listen to signs of physical hunger and eat only to the fullest,
- To distinguish between real hunger and non-hunger triggers for eating food,
- to engage your senses by recognizing colors, smells, sounds, textures and tastes,
- learning to cope with food-related guilt and anxiety,
- eating to preserve overall health and well-being,
- to recognize the effects of food on emotion and shape,
- to appreciate his food,

These things enables you to replace automatic thoughts and reactions with more conscious, healthier responses.

Why should we try to eat carefully?

Today's fast-paced people have plenty of food choices.

Beyond that, distractions have shifted from eating habits to televisions, computers and smartphones.

Eating food, often done quickly, has become a mindless move. This can be problematic, because it can take up to 20 minutes for your brain to realize you're full.

If you eat too fast, the saturation signal may not come on until you have eaten too much.

By eating carefully, you regain your attention and slow down intentionally, not automatically.

Moreover, by increasing your perception of physical hunger and saturation cues, you can distinguish between emotional and real eating, physical hunger.

In addition, even if you are not necessarily hungry, you will increase your awareness of triggers that want to eat.

Knowing your triggers, creating a space between them and your response, you can give you time and freedom to choose how to react.

Careful eating and weight loss

It is known that most weight loss programs do not work in the long run.

Approximately 85% of people with weight-losing obesity return to their initial weight in a few years or gain weight.

Excessive eating, emotional eating, and weight gain after successful weight loss have been associated with weight gain again.

Chronic exposure into stress may also play a major role in overeating and obesity.

Most studies agree that eating carefully helps you lose weight by changing your eating behavior and reducing stress.

Among people with obesity who underwent a 6-week careful eating group seminar, the average weight loss during the seminar and 12-week follow-up period was 4 kg.

Another 6-month seminar resulted at an average weight loss of 12 kg - no weight was recovered within the next 3 months.

By changing your thoughts about food, negative emotions that may be associated with eating are replaced by awareness, self-control and positive emotions

Considering unwanted eating behaviors, your chances of success in long-term weight loss increase.

Careful eating and eating

Over-eating involves eating a large amount of food in a short period of time, unwise and uncontrolled.

It has been associated with eating disorders and weight gain. One research showed that almost 70% of people with eating disorders were obese.

Careful eating can greatly reduce the severity and frequency of eating sections

Many people find it necessary to attend a seminar, online course or workshop on awareness or mindful eating.

However, there are various simple ways to get started, which can provide powerful benefits on their own:

- Eat more slowly and don't rush through your meals.
- Chew well.
- Turn off the TV and do not distract your phone by holding it during your meal.
- Eat quietly.
- Focus on how food makes you feel.
- Stop eating when you know you're saturated.

- Ask yourself why you are eating, whether you are really hungry, and whether the food you choose is healthy.
- First of all, it's a good idea to choose a meal a day to focus on these points.

Once you hang it, mindfulness will become more natural. Then you can focus on applying these habits into more meals.

Benefits Of Mindful Food

We live in a very fast world nowadays. Most people, maybe you too, eat in between, in a hurry, a quick bite here, a quick bite there, eat during a meeting (breakfast, lunch and dinner meetings). You do not allow yourself the time to enjoy your food. You may also recognize this: at home you are also eating in front of the TV. Your attention is completely distracted from what you are doing. If afterwards I would ask you: "What did you eat, what was the taste like?" I wonder if you could say what the different tastes were.

Today's children go a step further. Appen and mobiles while eating? Scrolling and multitasking while eating? This seems to be very normal for both adults and children. What you do not realize is that you completely ignore your digestion and enjoyment. The pleasure of and the gratitude for the food is completely gone.

Mindfulness not only applies to eating, but also to doing the dishes, brushing your teeth, showering and washing, driving, etc.

Benefits Of Mindful Eating

1. Improvement of your senses

It is not just about your taste and smell senses. Mindful living is connecting with sensory experiences in the moment, observing and connecting. Experience it in the broadest sense. See what the food looks like, observe the colors and patterns, hear the food (some foods also belong), feel the different textures.

Listen carefully to the sounds of the food, at a certain point you know what is normal and what is not normal. You will notice that different types of food make different sounds, both before you eat it and when eating it. At the smell of the food, you will notice that your mucous membranes respond to the odor.

Mindful eating is a good way to expand your awareness. You will also be able to benefit from it in daily life. You will discover strange reactions sooner, you will be unconsciously sharper and respond appropriately and appropriately. How you experience your life and how you live your life changes marked and unnoticed.

2. Enjoy the taste

If you eat your food greedily, there is no time to smell and taste and let everything go through you. Food should also give a feeling of satisfaction. Chew slowly and much so that the food is better absorbed into the body. Put down your fork, spoon and knife while you chew gently. Feel the food in your mouth, observe it, experience it and enjoy taste and smell, how it feels, how it reacts. Be completely in the now with what you are doing.

Drooling is now very appropriate. Due to the liquids that are released in the mouth, digestion starts in the oral cavity. The nutrients are already included here. Asians eat with smacking sounds where air is sucked in. This increases the sensation of the food. With us in the "civilized" world, this is only permitted with wine.

As said, put down that fork, and also the cell phone, turn off the TV and radio, don't talk for a moment. Put all your attention in the food. When you put all your attention and awareness into the food, you create appreciation for food, a different relationship with food. You will find that the food has never been so delicious. You will feel grateful. Also grateful for the people who made it possible for it to end up on your plate.

3. Eat like a bird, eat smaller portions

By taking small snacks, chewing well and enjoying it, you will take longer (see point 4). Optionally, take a teaspoon instead of a spoon, a dessert fork or chopsticks, a breakfast plate instead of a dinner plate. If you eat unconsciously, quickly, you tend to eat much more and much more often than necessary. By eating mindfully you will only eat what is needed to feel saturated.

The hormones, nervous system and brain need about 20 minutes to pass on a feeling of satiety. You will experience the feeling of being satisfied and satisfied. You become aware of your physical sensations. In addition, you feel proud of yourself that you have done very well again.

For people who want to lose weight, there are even more benefits. Further in this blog (second part) I will also mention it: control, control, trusting yourself, eating based on your internal needs and more.

4. Mindful eating helps with better absorption of nutrients

By eating small bites, chewing well, the nutrients in the food are released better. That is why your body absorbs better. This unquestionably promotes your health and stamina.

5. Mindful food creates peace

By taking time for eating and being mindful for food, time slows down and you relax. By being mindful, you forget all the hectic pace of the world. You create calmness and space within yourself. You are more focused on yourself in the moment. And you have created an environment in which you are not distracted. This is also being transmitted in all areas of life, so you will experience more well-being. The absorption of nutrients, satiety, appreciation and happiness become part of your awareness and well-being.

Another advantage is that you do not quickly serve a second time. You are fully aware of your body, you know what you need and what you don't. You feel it. Some people hear it and others see it. Your sense of or your vision of being saturated has improved. Moreover, you will no longer find pleasure in damaging your body and mind.

Mindful And Healthy Living: Tips

These five tips will get you on your way to more attentive eating habits:

Avoid distractions while eating

We often combine food with other activities. For example, television keeps many Belgian families company during meals.

Only 53 percent of Belgian children never watch TV during breakfast. 74 percent never look at lunch, and 59 percent never look at dinner. Children from vulnerable families - whose parents are less well educated - watch TV more often during the three main meals.

Are you distracted while eating? Then you eat more. Research shows that you eat 10 percent more if you watch TV or listen to the radio during lunch. That effect remains palpable, because you also eat more during the rest of the day. How is that possible? Because of the distraction during eating, your brain does not fully register that you are eating. As a result, you pay less attention to your feeling of satiety, you eat more and you run the risk of recovering. So choose food or your other task, but do not combine them.

So make sure that there is as little distraction as possible during eating: avoid screen time (while watching TV, tablet, mobile phone, computer, etc.), reading, calling, driving, cycling or busy conversations.

Adjust your portions

Do you want to eat healthier? Then take your portions:

- Eat smaller portions.
- Take smaller bites. This way you experience more taste stimuli and eat less.
- Decide in advance on how much you want to eat or drink. And put away the packaging again.

For example: put some nuts in a bowl and then put the rest away before you start eating.

This way you avoid eating or drinking directly from the package. Because then you eat or drink more than you want or need.

Eat three main meals (breakfast, lunch, dinner) and a maximum of three snacks.

For example: do not automatically taste cheese or sausage in the supermarket.

For example: do not eat a cookie at work every time you walk past the cookie jar.

Avoid eating because food happens to come your way. Because then you eat unknowingly. Moreover, you usually do not enjoy it that way.

Eat slowly and chew thoroughly

By eating slowly, you pay more attention to your feeling of satiety. A lot of chewing helps you to eat more slowly.

Use your senses

Focus on what your senses tell you while eating. Pay attention to smell and color, texture and taste. That way you eat more consciously and attentively. Do you get fewer sensory sensations? Then you probably ate enough.

Pause while eating

By interrupting your meal, you will eat more slowly. This makes you more alert to your feeling of satiety. Such a break also gives you the chance to consciously decide whether you want to eat more or not. Laying down your cutlery is a good way to insert such a break.

Mindful food: seven types of hunger

By eating mindful you can see why you eat. We distinguish seven types of hunger. Each species is linked to a body part and stands for a specific reason to eat.

- Ooghonger: you get hungry by seeing food or seeing others eat.

For example: a commercial about a new type of pudding

- Nose hunger: you feel like eating by smelling it.

For example: the smell of French fries when you walk past a deep fryer

- Mouth hunger: you crave certain tastes, sensations and textures.

For example: you want something fresh or sweet, or want to bite or chew on something.

- Stomach hunger: your stomach indicates that it is empty.
- Body hunger: your body indicates that it needs food.

For example: the shaking due to a low blood sugar level.

- Main hunger: you listen to your habits, rules and thoughts about food.

For example: "It is 12 o'clock: time to eat, because I do that every day."

or "Those chips are bad for me, I can't eat them."

- Harthonger: you eat because of your emotions or because of stress.

Do you want to eat something? First find out what kind of hunger it is, and consider whether food is the real answer to your needs. In this way you become more aware of your eating behavior and you respond less to automatic pilot.

Mindful food: dealing with negative feelings

By eating mindful, your eating behavior becomes less impulsive. It is an additional tool to break unhealthy eating habits. The means par excellence for tackling emo food.

Emo eating is a coping mechanism to suppress negative feelings. Eventually that becomes a habit that you no longer think about. With mindfulness you break that vicious circle. You consciously deal with the negative feelings, and you turn that awareness into a coping mechanism.

Mindfulness also causes a significant decrease in food cravings in overweight or obese people. The strategies that work best are based on acceptance. It is important to accept the cravings without trying to change, control or avoid them.

Both mindfulness and self-regulation provide you with concrete tools for independently controlling your eating behavior and permanently changing your eating habits. The two strategies each start from a different perspective.

Mindfulness focuses on accepting negative feelings.

Self-regulation changes feelings by setting goals and taking action.

How to eat healthy? Exercises

In her book Relaxed eating: with attention to a balanced eating pattern (2015), Rita Zeelenberg anticipates ten steps to eat in a relaxed way. She gives a number of concrete exercises for each step.

Self-test

The self-test below also comes from her book: you check how relaxed you eat. Answer the eight statements below with 'true' or 'false':

- I know the amount of calories for most things I eat.
- If someone treats, I always say no.
- I eat regularly without knowing why.
- I eat in company in a different way than when I am alone.
- I often worry about what I ate afterwards.
- I often eat in a rush because I am busy.
- Once the package of cookies is open, it must be empty.
- Sometimes I no longer know what is healthy for me and what is not.

Did you answer many statements with 'where'? Then there is a great priviledge that your food will be less relaxed:

You often think about it beforehand: 1, 2 and 8.

Afterwards you doubt: 5 and 7.

The circumstances often influence how you eat: 3, 4 and 6.

If you scored high on the aspects above, then it is best to examine your eating pattern.

The hunger meter

The hunger meter is another exercise from the book. Indicate how hungry you are every hour for a few days, with a figure from 1 to 10. 1 stands for overcrowded, 10 stands for starving. Use the description below as a guide:

- I feel crowded, almost nauseous. My stomach is set up and can even hurt.
- My stomach is uncomfortably full, I have eaten too much.
- I am satisfied and my stomach feels full.
- I just ate something and that feels good, but something can be added.
- I no longer feel hungry and reasonably saturated.
- My stomach is grinding a bit, it would feel good to eat something.
- I am hungry and want a hearty meal.
- I am very hungry: I feel that my body really needs food.
- Hunger makes me feel restless, it occupies my mind.
- I'm famished. My stomach is so empty and I feel weak and energy-free.

Eat a full portion at grade 7 and stop eating at 3.

Up to the age of five you feel your innate sense of satiety: you know when to eat and when to stop. As you get older, it becomes more difficult. You will then be confronted with temptations from outside and you will, for example, have to completely empty your plate. With the hunger meter learn to pay attention to your hunger feeling again.

Another Method On How To Convert Eating With Mindfulness Into A Diet

Diets have to do with war, with war on calories, with war on eating certain foods, with war on the natural wisdom of our body. Science has shown that diets are not effective and that they are quite harmful to health, involve subjecting tremendous emotional and physical stress that causes a defensive response of our body and the universe of microorganisms that live in our body.

Lilia Graue made us palpable that "mindful eating is rapidly increasing in popularity as a common sense approach to solve a large number of food-related problems and that it has been especially effective in breaking the cycle" eat-repent-repeat ”That so often results from food restriction. Unfortunately, many people who are getting on the food train with mindfulness do not understand the subtle but significant differences between this practice and the typical diets. They filter the concepts of food with mindfulness through the already established paradigm of diets and simply turn food with mindfulness into one more diet - with the same predictable results! »

Lilia echoed a wonderful article by Michelle May, MD that is reproduced below:

To highlight some of the common mistakes, here is how to convert eating with full attention to dieting - and what to do instead.

1. Make new diet-type rules such as "Only eat when you are hungry" and "Always for when you are full."

Why: Feel guilty if you eat when you are not hungry or judge yourself for eating after a 5 or 6 year? It is different from dieting. This restrictive way of eating will lead you to the same cycle of eating-repenting-repeating.

Instead: When you feel like eating, pause and ask yourself "Am I hungry?" - not to decide if you have permission to eat, but to recognize why you want to eat. With this type of awareness, you can freely choose whether to eat or not.

2. Think about eating with full attention in terms of "Tips and tricks" instead of how a practice.

Why: Tips like "Chew each bite for 20 times" do not lead to increased awareness, only to boredom! And while we are all used to headlines such as "5 Tricks to Not Deviate from Your Diet" that "magical" approach in the short term leads to short-term behaviors.

Instead: Unlike dieting, which typically becomes more difficult to sustain over time, eating with full attention becomes more natural with practice. By learning how to pay attention to your physical sensations, thoughts and feelings over time, you discover that you have an internal expert that naturally guides you towards balance, variety and moderation.

3. Use food with mindfulness to resist eating the foods you crave.

Why: What you resist persists!

Instead: Mindfulness teaches you to let whatever you notice simply be. You may notice that you fancy a favorite food from your childhood. Instead of resisting it, you get curious (or) about craving. How does the craving feel? What, specifically, do you want about that food? What associations do you have with that food? Do these associations give you any clues about your underlying needs? How would it feel to eat that food? How would it feel if you don't eat it? And so on.

4. Allow yourself to be forgiving with your favorite treats by tasting only one or two bites.

Why: This seemingly permissive advice remains restrictive! When you have to have "permission" to eat a favorite food being "forgiving" as long as you follow specific rules, these subtle messages feed an unconscious feeling of judgment and deprivation that can paradoxically lead to overeating.

Instead: Do not put arbitrary limits on food that ultimately lead to "cheating" and feeling guilty. Mindful feeding helps you trust your inner expert to eat what you love and love what you eat.

5. Focus on losing weight.

Why: A simple definition of mindfulness is the judgment-free awareness of the present moment. You cannot change your weight at the present time, so focusing on weight loss keeps you focused on something that is in the future.

Instead of this: Become more aware of your physical signs of hunger and satiety and how you feel when you eat different types and amounts of food. Tune in to the appearance, aromas, flavors and textures of the foods you select. Notice how you feel when you move your body. Use the signals from your body to practice self-care, such as resting when your body is tired, pausing when you feel stressed (or), connecting with others when you feel boredom or loneliness, etc. Moment to moment, note the effects of the choices you make and allow that awareness to affect the choices you make.

Are You 0f Thinking Going On A Diet? Better Do Not Do It

In these days of the beginning of the year we propose new purposes, things that we want to change. At this time of the year along with spring with the "bikini operation" are two moments in which we think that perhaps it is time to go on a diet.

If you are considering of going on a diet you should know that diets are not very effective. In 95% of the cases, if you manage to lower your kiss, after having made this effort, this war to the kilos, it is very likely that you will increase what you lost and add an average of 3 kg more to the balance according to different scientific publications * .

This situation is not surprising because when we go on a diet we give the message to our body, genetically programmed for scarcity, that we are in a time of shortage and we have to put ourselves in saving mode. This means that our body will begin to save money to spend less energy. The restrictions to which we submit to our body cause us to lose weight, but when we leave the diet, our body receives the message that there is abundance again, and it is time to accumulate and accumulate by the time new times of scarcity return.

We know that hunger is something that has to do with the nutrition of the body, but also with the nutrition of the heart, and many times when we go on a diet, we take off all those foods that we associate at certain moments of our vital history with love and Loving nutrition Prohibitions exalt desire, and when those prohibitions cease we tend to abuse what we wanted. When we go on a diet we deprive ourselves of those cookies that our mother or our grandmother made us lovingly, of that dessert they gave us when we were sick or of that dish that we enjoyed so dearly in family celebrations. When we leave the diet, the desire for this type of food could be so great that when we eat them again, we do it in excess and in an unconscious way. In this way this war to the kg, a form of violence and denial of the nutritional needs of our being, is usually destined to fail. The Buddha said that hate is only extinguished with love, not with hate. In the case of weight problems the same thing will happen to us, only love, conscience, generosity and compassion can lead us to overcome the problems we have with weight.

One way to relate lovingly to weight problems is with love. In Buddhism, unconditional, metta love is a positive emotion. This society so tinged with sensitivity when it speaks of love usually evokes romantic love as an example; But this love is a conditioned love: I love you if you love me, if you don't love me, I ignore you or even hate you. There is also another type of love, which is an unconditional love that emerges from the depths of the human being. In the tradition the example of the deeply unconditional love that springs in a mother or a father towards the son is given; Regardless of the actions of that son or daughter, whether clumsy or skilled, do things better or worse, there is usually an unconditional love base. This is the kind of unconditional love, metta, that we can cultivate towards ourselves and towards our relationship with food.

Unfortunately, many people feel they need to give up, condemn or make war on certain foods to achieve greater well-being. And it is very frequent that every time we make more and more lists of foods to eliminate to achieve longevity, happiness, success and the recognition of all those around you. It is not really necessary to give up these things to be happy and healthy.

The first step to be able to establish a love relationship with food is to know what that relationship with food is like, how our relationship with food is a cause of our suffering. The best method to get started on this path is by cultivating attention, developing mindfulness when eating , and establishing a loving relationship with our difficulty with food and what causes us discomfort, discomfort and suffering.

Many times we eat cookies not because we need sugar, flour or sesame, but because we need the love and love with which our mother prepared them. By cultivating awareness in our way of eating, we can see all those ingredients and cultivate a space for choice and decide if we really want to eat it or not, without judgment, without recrimination,

Our relationship with food can be very tortuous and can lead to suffering, guilt and much self-criticism and the best way to approach these problems is with compassion. Compassion is one of the essential nutrients for the heart. Compassion is as essential to the spirit as water and food are to the body.

There are two aspects to compassion. The first is the ability to feel pain and suffering without fear, with an open heart; the other is a quality of wisdom that sees this pain and suffering as a natural part of life.

Both aspects of compassion help to alleviate pain and suffering, that pain and suffering that manifests itself with weight gain on the scale, but also a great emotional weight. We all have our secrets, sorrows and something that causes us suffering. Metaphorically speaking, pain and emotional suffering, without conscious attention, is usually very difficult to swallow. The wisdom of compassion can make us see that suffering is part of life, just as hunger is part of appetite. We cannot always be full and satisfied. When we accept suffering and hunger, we can let it go. And through compassion a different level of fullness arises.

For now, now that the year starts, maybe it's time to leave behind. Leave violence and the war on food with diets behind. Leave the fight against food behind. Leave guilt and victimhood behind. Leaving fierce and ruthless self-criticism behind what we eat or how our body shape is. What we eat, the shape of our body does not determine our value as a person. Leave self-rejection and restriction behind.

Maybe it's time for a new true purpose. Stop making war on food and interact with love and awareness with it, and with compassion towards us with all our difficulties.

1. Deer square with apricots

Description

Apricots simply go great with fresh venison. The sweetness of the fruit blends well with the natural venison taste of the venison. A fast but delicious game.

Preparation

1. Preheat the oven to 100 degrees Celsius. Wash deer boxes, dry and parry. Season with salt and pepper. Heat oil and butter in a pan. Put rosemary sprigs in the pan. Roast venison from all sides well. Remove from the pan and place inside a fireproof mold. Put the meat in the

oven and cook the meat gently for about 15 to 20 minutes.

2. Peel the apricots and cut into quarters. Slowly heat the sugar in a pan and caramelise. Add butter. Deglaze with white wine and let the sugar dissolve. Add apricots and simmer for about five minutes. Add the cumin and season with salt and pepper. Remove half of the apricots from the brew and set aside. Cook the remaining apricots gently and then puree to a thick sauce.

3. Remove stag-boxes from the oven and let them rest a bit. Serve the apricots and fruit sauce with the meat.

2. Wild boar steak from the Beefer with fruity crust

Description

Prepare a venison steak in a minute - can you? In Beefer at 900 degrees Celsius, the meat cooks in a few seconds. A crust of apple and breadcrumbs gives the meat a fruity-crispy topping.

Preparation

1. Cut the meat, for example from the wild boar leg (upper dish), into slices of about three centimeters. Season the boar steaks with salt, a little sugar and let rest briefly.

2. Cut a zucchini in half for the side dish and cut into bite-sized pieces with the paprika. Fry a chopped onion in olive oil, add these glazed, zucchini, peppers and all the cherry tomatoes. Season with salt, pepper and fresh herbs. Did the vegetables take color, deglaze with a sip of red wine and let reduce. Then stir in a tablespoon of cream and bring to a boil over low heat. Ready is the creamy vegetables.

3. For the steak crust, mix a cup of breadcrumbs with a dash of olive oil, a dash of lemon and a half, very small diced apple and fresh chopped herbs. Season with salt

and pepper. The mixture should be slightly sticky, slightly sour and fruity taste.

4. Heat the Beefer. Put the steaks at the highest level in the top slot and roast for a few seconds, turning once and heating the other side until the meat has a brown crust. It should not be charred.

5. Firmly top the steaks with the mixture for about two centimeters and press lightly. Now place in the bottom slot of the Beefer and heat until the crust takes on good color and becomes crispy.

3. Boar Salsiccia With Sweet Potato And Bean Vegetables

Description

This hearty casserole is really "smart", as relevant cooking magazines would probably write. The culprits are the sweet potatoes and the vegetables - and the wild bratwurst - that has what it takes to become a new favorite recipe.

Preparation

1. Preheat the oven to 230 degrees Celsius. Peel sweet potatoes and cut into small cubes (about 2 cm in size). Peel the onion and cut into eighths. Peel garlic and crush lightly.

2. Put the sweet potatoes in a casserole dish and mix well with the olive oil. Spread onion, garlic and thyme twigs over it. Distribute sausages on top and put the casserole dish in the hot oven for about 20 minutes.

3. Drain the beans and drain. Wash chard and cut into strips. Remove the casserole from the oven, remove the sprigs of thyme and peel off the leaves a little.

4. Remove the sausage from the casserole and set it aside. Put the broth over the casserole and stir in the beans and chard. Finally, put the sausages back on the vegetables. Put the casserole in the oven for another ten minutes.

4. Deer pie

Description

Still looking for a hearty, but unusual festive meal? We have changed the Irish Pie a bit, wild and regionalized. Deer meat from the local hunt and a black country beer from the region round off the hearty pate.

Preparation

1. Parry the shoulder of the deer and cut the meat into bite-sized pieces.

2. Fry the meat in oil in a large roasting pan until well roasted, season with salt, pepper and rosemary and put aside.

3. Sprinkle a piece of butter in the same roasting pan and sauté the chopped onions. Then add the finely chopped vegetables and sauté. Now deglaze with the beer and put the meat back in the roasting pan.

4. Close the roasting pan and place in the pre-baked oven for two and a half hours at 180 degrees Celsius. Stir after half of the cooking time.

5. Now grind 100 grams of cheddar and stir.

6. Grease a baking dish and lay out with the puff pastry. Spread meat-vegetable mixture on top and sprinkle with the remaining cheddar. Brush the edge of the dough with a beaten egg yolk and put on a second layer of puff pastry and lightly press.

7. Cut the top of the dough with a knife, brush with egg yolk and place the casserole on the bottom rail of the oven at 180 degrees Celsius for 45 minutes.

8. Butter peas and a cool black beer go well with that.

5. Chicken soup with ginger

Ingredients

- Two cooked chicken steaks and chopped
- Four tablespoons of cooked and chopped carrots
- 3 cups chicken water
- A tablespoon of oil
- A small piece of ginger (not much bigger than a hazelnut), unless you love the spicy taste of this root

- A grated onion
- A garlic kernel, chopped
- One tablespoon of cornstarch
- Small salt

The preparations

First, onions and garlic must be fried in the oil. Incidentally, the carrot should be cooked with two cups of chicken broth in the blender. Next, this cream should be added onions and garlic porridge. At that time, the ginger had added the recipe, and everything had to cook for a few minutes.

Meanwhile, the cornstarch in the second broth must be dissolved from the rest of the chicken shell. Currently it is continuously cooked and stirred until it thickens. At the last moment, the chicken is incorporated, the salt tasted and served immediately.
Yield: 4 servings

Calories per serving: about 150 calories

6. Grilled knives

Ingredients:

Navajas 12

Garlic cloves 2

Parsley to taste

Extra virgin olive oil (a splash)

For 1-2 person

Preparation:

To thoroughly clean the knives, they are placed in a container with water and a little salt and left there for several hours so that the knives expel the sand they contain inside.

Then they are removed and washed with fresh water. Put the iron to heat and pour a splash of oil that is then removed with a paper. When the iron is hot, place the knives on the plate, seasoning them with a little salt. It will be enough to leave them on the plate for two minutes so that they are at their point.

While the knives are cooked, the garlic cloves and parsley are well blended, mixing evenly. When removing the knives from the iron, place a teaspoon of that mixture on each plate and place it inside the slow cooker.

Nutritional Facts

Amount per serving:

Calories: 2.13

Total fat: 8.6g

Carbohydrates: 17.3g

Fiber: 1.3g

Protein: 17.9g

7. Mackerel steaks in butter

Health benefits of Mackerel steaks in butter One thing that most doctors, dietitians and health professionals are generally able to agree upon across the board is that adding fish to your diet comes with some major benefits to health. In fact, the American Heart Association actually recommends including at least two servings of fatty fish in your weekly diet to help enhance heart health. Tuna and herring fish in terms of nutrition is mackerel fish, a super-nutritious type of fish that's practically bursting with protein, omega-3 fatty acids and micronutrients.

Ingredients

- Bunch of dill: 1
- Onions (small): 2
- Oil: 2 tbsp. soup
- Lemon juice: 2
- Salt
- Pepper
- For lemon butter:
- Butter: 200 g
- Lemon juice: 2
- Fresh cream: 10 cl
- Salt
- Cayenne pepper

Preparation

1. Empty, cut and clean the fish by your fishmonger. Peel the onions and cut them into thin slices; wash the dill. Season the inside of the fish and add the dill sprigs.
2. Preheat the oven to 240 ° C. Cut 4 rectangles of parchment paper (about 22 x 24 cm). Place on each a few slices of onions then add the mackerel, incise their skin; sprinkle with olive oil and lemon juice. Close the wrappers tightly while rolling the edges.
3. Prepare the lemon butter: put the cream in a saucepan and reduce to 2/3; add the butter gradually in small pieces. Stir with a whisk over a very soft fire. Top with lemon juice and season with salt and cayenne pepper; keep the sauce warm in a bain-marie.
4. Put the wrappers on a plate and cook them in the oven for 8 minutes. Serve the wrappers directly on a plate and let the guests open them themselves to smell the cooking fragrance.

8. Crispy Chicken Thighs with Bacon

Ingredient

- Four chicken drumsticks (s)
- Eight slices/ s Bacon, about 100 g
- Herbs, Mediterranean (rosemary, thyme, oregano, lavender)
- sea salt
- 1 tbsp. olive oil

Cooking time: approx. 50 min

Calorie: about 300 kcal

Preparation

1. Preheat oven at 180 ° C (160 ° C convection). Wash the chicken thighs and pat dry.
2. Heat the olive oil in a frying pan (if oven suitable) and fry the legs from all sides. Remove from the pan, season well all around (freshly chopped Mediterranean herbs or a high-quality dry mix) and salt. Then wrap with two slices of bacon, if necessary fix with wooden toothpicks, roast again in the still hot pan from above and below. Be careful when turning.
3. Put the pan inside the oven for 30 minutes and add a touch of olive oil if necessary. If there is no pan suitable for cooking, place the legs on the oven rack and push a sheet of baking paper under it as a safety catch, after half the time turn the thighs. Serve hot!

It fits a light raw food salad.

Tip:

Do not use a casserole dish (used in the photo only for decorative purposes). In this, the thighs swim too much in their juice and are therefore not crispy.

Nutritional Information per Piece

- 300 kcal
- 16 g fat (of which 6 g total fat)
- KH 600 mg
- Protein 40 g

9. Grilled Marinated Flank Steak, Holistic Recipe

Number of portions: 6

Ingredients

2 pounds of flank steak

1/3 cup olive oil

2 garlic cloves, chopped

2 tablespoons of red wine vinegar

1/3 cup of liquid amino

1/4 cup of honey

1/2 teaspoon freshly ground black pepper

Preparation

1. Score the surface of the steak by slicing it into 1/4-inch deep knife cuts 1/2-inch across the meat grain.

2. Mix the remaining ingredients and pour over the steak to get a marinade.

3. Apply well and refrigerate for at least 2 hours or overnight.

4. Preheat the grill for medium heat.

5. Using olive oil soaked in a paper towel; coat the grill of your grill with olive oil.

6. Take the steak out of the marinade and sprinkle it with salt and pepper. This will create a crust on the steak.

7. Put the steak on the hot grill and grill for 4-6 minutes per side, depending on how you like your steak. Flank steak should be served medium in size for best results. Well done would make tough meat.

8. Remove the grill and cover with foil for 10 minutes to seal all juices.

9. Cut very thin slices against the grain and make sure the slices are wide.

10. Take the excess marinade, bring to a boil and cook for a few minutes and serve over the flank steak.

10.Grilled chicken with ranch sauce

Preparation: 30 min

Baking: 1 h 25 min

Maceration: 12 h

Servings: 4

Ingredients

Chicken

1 lb. chicken (4 lb.)

10 ml (2 teaspoons) salt

5 ml (1 teaspoon) of garlic powder

½ lemons

1 recipe of ranch vinaigrette

Salad

4 celery stalks, minced

1 bulb of fennel, finely chopped

1 green onion, chopped

30 ml (2 tablespoons) chopped fennel leaves

30 ml (2 tablespoons) of olive oil

15 ml (1 tablespoon) lemon juice

Preparation

Chicken

1. On a work surface, using the chef's knife or kitchen scissors, remove the bone from the back of the chicken. Flip the chicken and cut in half in the center of the breasts. Place the pieces in a large glass dish. Sprinkle chicken skin with salt and garlic powder. Rub the outside and rthen inside of the chicken with the cut part of the lemon. Thoroughly

coat with 1/2 cup (125 mL) ranch vinaigrette. Cover and refrigerate 12 hours.

2. Preheat half of the barbecue at high power. Oil the grill on the off side.
3. Drain the meat. Place the chicken on the off-the-grill section, skin side on the grill. Close the barbecue lid. Bake 45 minutes while maintaining a temperature of 200 ° C (400 ° F). Return the chicken and continue cooking for 35 minutes or until a thermometer inserted in the thigh, without touching the bone, indicates 180 ° F (82 ° C) maintaining a temperature of 200 ° C (400 ° F).). Finish cooking on the lit section of the barbecue to mark the chicken.

Salad

4. Meanwhile, in a bowl, mix all ingredients. Salt and pepper.

Cut the chicken into pieces. Serve with the salad and the rest of the ranch vinaigrette.

11.Potato gratin with chicken and guacamole

Serves: 4

Ingredients

4 potatoes

1 large chicken breast

Egg and breadcrumbs for breading

Salt

Ground pepper

Sweet or spicy paprika

Grated cheese

Guacamole

Instructions

Peel the potatoes, cut the cane.

Add some threads of oil, salt, ground pepper and paprika.

Mix well and put in the cuvette of the Actifry.

We take the Actifry and select 30 minutes.

Cut the chicken into strips, pass through egg and breadcrumbs.

We paint with extra virgin olive oil.

We take the Airfryer and select 30 minutes, 180 degrees.

When the potatoes are ready we pass them to a baking sheet.

On the potatoes we place the chicken, which if it is very large, we can chop.

We cover everything with a layer of grated cheese.

We take to the oven, 180 degrees, about 15 minutes.

We serve with a little guacamole above.

12.Chicken with Provencal herbs in Airfryer with potatoes

Serves: 2

Ingredients

4 potatoes

2 chicken hindquarters

Provencal herbs

Salt

Ground pepper

Extra virgin olive oil

Instructions

Peel the potatoes and cut into slices.

Pepper and put on the grid of the base Airfryer.

We impregnate the chicken well with oil, salt and pepper and put some Provencal herbs.

We place the chicken on the potatoes.

We take the grill to the bucket of the Airfryer and put inside.

We select 170 degrees 40 minutes.

We turn the chicken and leave 15 more minutes.

We serve

13.Ham croquettes in Airfryer with yogurt sauce salad

Serves: 4

Ingredients

1 bag of ham croquettes

1 bag of mixed salad

1 handful of nuts

Salad Yogurt Sauce

Salt

Instructions

We wash the lettuce and drain well.

We put the croquettes in the basket of the Airfryer and paint with a little oil.

We select 20 minutes, 180 degrees.

We spread the salad between four dishes.

We distribute the croquettes between the four dishes.

We add a stream of yogurt sauce in each salad.

We decorate with peeled walnuts.

We serve

14. Torrijas in Airfryer

Serves: 8

Ingredients

For the bread: 500 gr of flour

25 gr of oil

300 gr of water

25 gr of fresh bread yeast

12 gr of salt

For French toast: Milk and cinnamon or milk and sweet wine

Eggs

Honey

Instructions

The first thing is to make bread a day before. We put in the Masterchef Gourmet the ingredients of the bread and knead 1 minutes at speed 1.

We allow the dough rise for 1 hour and knead again 1 minute at speed 1.

Remove the dough and divide into 4 portions. We make a ball and spread like a pizza.

Roll up to make a small loaf of bread and let rise 1 hour or so.

We take to the oven and bake 40 minutes, 200 degrees.

Let the bread cool on a rack and reserve for the next day.

Cut the bread into slices and reserve.

You have to prepare the milk to wet the slices of bread, for this we put the milk to heat, like 500 ml or so with a cinnamon stick or the same milk with a glass of sweet wine, as we like. When the milk has started to boil, remove from heat and let cool.

We beat the eggs.

We place a rack on a plate and we dip the slices of bread in the cold milk, then in the beaten egg and pass to the rack with the plate underneath to release the excess liquid.

We put the slices of bread in the bucket of the Airfryer, in batches, not piled up, and we take the Airfryer, 180 degrees, 10 minutes each batch.

When we have all the slices passed through the Airfryer, we put the honey in a casserole, like 500 gr, next to 1 small glass of water and 4 tablespoons of sugar.

When the honey begins to boil, we lower the heat and pass the slices of bread through the honey.

We place in a fountain and the rest of the honey we put it on top, bathing again the French toast.

Ready our French toast, when they cool, they can already be eaten.

15.Peppers stuffed with tortillas in Airfryer

Serves: 6

Ingredients

6 large green Italian peppers

4 potatoes

1 onion

4 eggs

Extra virgin olive oil

Salt

Instructions

Peel the potatoes and cut them into flakes.

Peel the onion and cut into fine julienne.

We put in a large pan a bottom of extra virgin olive oil and add the potatoes along with the onion. We put salt and cover to simmer, with its own steam.

Stir occasionally.

When the potatoes are tender, we go to a bowl where we will have the previously beaten eggs.

Let's bind well, we rectify salt.

Cut the tail of the peppers and by the mouth that remains, removing the seeds inside, fill with the tortilla mixture.

We put the peppers, inclined so that the filling does not come out, in the basket of the Airfryer.

We select 30 minutes, 160 degrees.

We take out of the basket and serve as is or cut into slices.

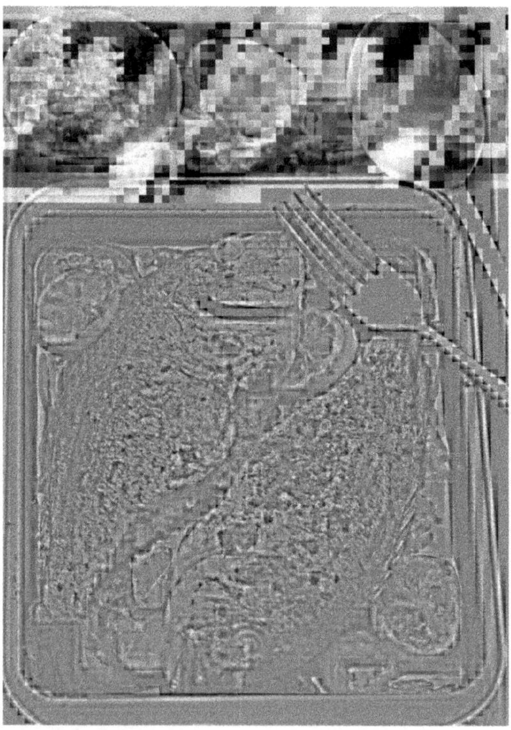

16.Baked sea bream in Lebanese style

Ingredients:

For the dish:

1 kilogram of whole fish type bream, salmon or trout

1 teaspoon of salt

1 teaspoon of cumin

1 teaspoon sweet pepper (paprikas)

1 onion

1 lemon

2 bay leaves

3 tomatoes

For the sauce:

3 cloves of garlic

1 tablespoon coriander seeds

1/2 teaspoon of salt

100 g of onion

1/2 bunch of green coriander

65 g of tahini (sesame puree)

1 lemon or about 50 ml of lemon juice

1/2 glass of vegetable oil (sunflower or olive)

10 g pine nuts

25 g chopped walnuts

1/2 to 1 teaspoon of fine cayenne pepper powder (according to taste)

1 pinch of pepper

Preparation:

1. Wash the fish; rub both sides with a teaspoon of salt, sweet pepper, and cumin. In a large baking tray, add the onion, tomatoes, and lemon sliced and put the fish and bay leaf. Add 1 glass of water. Sprinkle with a drizzle of olive oil.

2. Heat up the oven to 180 ° C. Put the tray in the oven and cook for 20 minutes or 25 minutes depending on the type and thickness of the fish.

3. With a pestle, crush garlic, salt, and coriander seeds until coriander becomes powder. Set aside.

4. Minute an onion, finely chop green coriander and leave aside.

5. In a large bowl, pour tahini, lemon juice, and 100 ml water. Mix well until you obtain a homogeneous liquid, then reserve.

6. In a saucepan, add vegetable oil, heat over medium heat. Brown the pine nuts, drain them.

7. In the same saucepan and remaining oil, brown the chopped onion. Add green coriander, the garlic-cilantro mixture in seeds and chopped walnuts and pepper. Simmer another 10 minutes. Finally, add tahini, lemon, and water. Cook for about 10 minutes. 8. Add the chili, mix and remove from the heat. Leave this sauce aside for dressing.

To serve, place the fish on a large plate, decorate with slices of peppers, tomatoes or any other vegetable to give color. Put the sauce on the fish, and then scatter over the pine nuts.

Good realization and good tasting!

Nutritional Information

Potassium 967.12mg 28%

Carbohydrates 0g 0%

Dietary Fiber 0g 0%

Sugars 0g

17.Beef Dish with Bird Lettuce

Cooking time: More than 60 min

Ingredients

- Servings: 4
- 600 g boiled beef (cooked)
- 6 cl of Sherry Dry
- 2 carrots
- 2 turnips (yellow)
- 1/4 celeriac

- 4 tablespoons of chives (chopped)
- 600 ml of beef soup
- 10 sheets of gelatin
- Vegetable oil (for the form)
- Pepper (from the mill)
- Salt
- 200 g of bird's lettuce
- Pumpkinseed-pesto
- Chives (to sprinkle)

For The Marinade:

- 4 tablespoons of corn oil
- 3 tablespoons apple cider vinegar
- 2 tablespoons of beef soup
- Pinch of salt

Preparation

1. Boil the soup with 200 ml of water.
2. Add carrots, yellow turnips and celery and cook until soft. Remove from the soup, let cool and cut into 3 mm thick strips.
3. Soak the gelatin inside cold water, squeeze and add to the soup. Season well with sherry, salt and pepper and remove from Air fryer heat.

4. Spread the terrine mold with little oil, insert the plastic wrap lengthwise and smooth with kitchen paper.
5. Cut the top of the heated beef from the Air fryer (preferably with the bread slicer) into 2 mm thick slices, dip each slice into the still warm soup one at a time and line the shape with it. In doing so, arrange overlapping about 6 cm over the edge.
6. Pour in a little soup, sprinkle with chives, place the vegetable strips lengthways and top them dipped in soup. Repeat this process three times; Pour in the rest of the soup.
7. Press foil and refrigerate for 3 hours. For the marinade, mix all ingredients with a whisk and marinate the lettuce. Toss the terrine, remove the foil and cut into slices.
8. Arrange on chilled plates and garnish with the marinated lettuce. Drizzle with pumpkin seed pesto and sprinkle with chives.

Tip

Depending on the season, the vegetable inlay of the Sulz can be modified with radishes, asparagus or pickled mushrooms. Drizzled with apple cider vinegar and sprinkled with Fleur de sel and pepper, the Sulz tastes even spicier.

Nutrition Information

- 221kcal
- Fat: 13g
- Saturated fat: 7g
- Carbohydrates: 1g
- Protein: 23g

18.Keto stuffed avocados with smoked salmon

2 portions

Ingredients

- 2 avocados
- 175 g smoked salmon

- 175 ml fresh cream or mayonnaise
- Salt and pepper
- 2 tbsps. lemon juice (optional)

Instructions

1. Slice the avocados into half and remove the bone.
2. Put a spoonful of fresh cream in the hollow of the avocado and add smoked salmon on top.
3. Season to taste with little salt and sprinkle with lemon juice to give more flavor (and avoid the avocado acquires a brown color).

Advice

This ketogenic dish can be served with any other type of fatty fish, boiled, fried or smoked. It tastes better with a little fresh dill!

19.Salad with Avocado, Pineapple And Cucumbers

Time preparation: 25 min.

Servings: 4

Ingredients

1 sliced cucumber

3 slices of pineapple (pineapple)

1/2 red onion filleted

2 avocados (avocados)

1/3 cup olive oil

2 tbsp lemon juice

1 cdita salt

1 cdita pepper

Preparation

1. Cut the avocado and pineapple in medium cubes.
2. Subsequently cut the cucumber along, remove the seeds with a spoon and cut into slices.
3. Mix the above inside a bowl, add the red onion, salt, pepper and season with olive oil and lemon juice.

Nutritional information

- Calories: 90.2
- Total Fat: 4.6 g
- Dietary Fiber: 2.5 g
- Saturated Fat: 1.7 g

20.Mango and avocado salad

You will love the colors of this salad of mango, and avocado. The mixture makes it a vibrant and fun salad.

4 people

Time preparation: 10 minutes

Ingredients for 4 people

- 1 unit (s) of chopped Lettuce
- 1 pinch of Pepper
- 1 unit (s) of Avocado
- 1 unit (s) of Mango

- 1 tablespoon White wine vinegar
- 1 tablespoon of olive oil
- 2 tablespoon of chopped toasted almonds
- 2 tablespoon dried cranberries
- Salt

Preparation

1. Peel and chop the vegetables.

2. Put the lettuce, mango, avocado, almonds, and cranberries in a bowl.

3. On the other hand, mix the oil with the vinegar and add salt and pepper.

4. Pour over the salad and mix.

5. Serve on plates and enjoy.

Nutritional composition for 100 grs

Composition	Amount (gr)	CDR (%)
Kcalories	259.3	13.5%
Carbohydrates	19.59	6.3%
Proteins	4.15	8.7%

Fiber 5.77 19.2%

Fat 16.98 31.9%

21.Avocado and lettuce salad

2 people

Time preparation: 10 minutes

Ingredients for 2 people

- 1 unit (s) of Tomato cut
- 1 unit (s) of Lettuce
- 0.5 unit (s) of red pepper, diced julienne
- 1 pinch of Pepper
- 1 unit (s) of Avocado
- 2 tablespoon Nuez chopped (walnut crepes)

- 1 pinch of salt
- 2 tablespoon of Modena balsamic vinegar
- 2 tablespoon of lemon juice
- 1 pinch of extra virgin olive oil

Preparation

1. Wash the lettuce well and chop it.

2. Wash and chop the remaining ingredients such as the Tomato, red pepper or diced julienne, Avocado, Nuez chopped Modena balsamic vinegar.

3. Mix the lemon juice, vinegar, virgin oil, salt, and pepper. Then toss on the salad.

4. Remove and add the nuts (optional) to garnish.

Nutritional composition for 100 grs

Composition	Amount (gr)	CDR (%)
Kcalories	315.53	16.5%
Carbohydrates	10.8	3.5%
Proteins	6.55	13.7%
Fiber	7.55	25.2%

Fat 25.88 48.7%

22.Zucchini Spaghetti

1 person

Time preparation: 10 minutes

Ingredients for 1 person

1 unit (s) of zucchini

1 pinch of Herbamare herbal salt or normal salt

Preparation

1. Pass the zucchini ALONG by the large grater; nothing happens if it is cut in half because it is impossible to make it perfect.

2. When you have grated all the zucchini, Herbamare herbal salt or normal salt and prepare while your sauce so that the zucchini is losing water.

3. You can heat them in a pan, but raw tastes less and takes the flavor of what you throw to accompany.

4. Add the sauce with which you will combine it and serve it.

Nutritional composition for 100 grs.

Composition	Amount (gr)	CDR (%)
Kcalories	44.3	2.3%
Carbohydrates	3.85	1.2%
Proteins	3.58	7.5%
Fiber	3.04	10.1%
Fat	0.96	1.8%

23.Salad of red beans with guacamole

4 people

Time preparation: 30 minutes

Ingredients for 4 people

1 unit (s) of Tomato (medium)

1 unit (s) of Onion (half onion purple)

1 unit (s) of red pepper (medium)

1 pinch of Pepper

1 unit (s) of Limón

1 pinch of salt

1 unit (s) of Green pepper

250 grams of Azuki a pot (canned red beans already cooked)

1 tablespoon of extra virgin olive oil

1 unit (s) of fresh Guacamole Frutas Montosa (Mercadona) you can make it homemade too

1 small cup of sweet corn in a can

Preparation

1. Prepare the salad by mixing all the chopped ingredients such as Tomato, Onion, Limón, with the beans previously washed, Azuki and drained.
2. Dress with lemon juice and oil and season with salt and Green pepper.
3. Serve the salad with the guacamole and toast with toasted bread.

Nutritional composition for 100 grs.

Composition Amount (gr) CDR (%)

Kcalories 353.04 18.4%

Carbohydrates 42.06 13.5

Proteins 14.75 30.8%

Fiber 13.82 46.1%

Fat 10.33 19.4%

24.Vegetarian recipe

Time preparation: 1 hour

Ingredients:

1 cup of green beans

2 carrots

Sweet corn

Cooked rice

A teaspoon of mustard

A little honey

Olive oil

A handful of cooked chickpeas

Three or four chopped pistachios

Preparations:

1. You have to mix some green beans and some boiled or steamed carrots, along with sweet corn and cooked rice.
2. To dress it, mix a teaspoon of mustard with a little honey and olive oil. And if you want to turn it into a complete and balanced single dish, you can add a handful of cooked chickpeas and three or four chopped pistachios. Besides being delicious, this vegetarian recipe is one of the best meals to take to work.

Nutritional information

- Calories: 111
- Total Fat: 2g
- Saturated Fat: 1g

- Cholesterol: 10mg
- Sodium: 58mg
- Carbohydrates: 19g
- Fiber: 0 g
- Sugar: 18 g
- Calcium: 15%
- Iron: 0%

25.Raw Vegetables. Chopped Salad

Preparation time: 15 minutes

Total time: 15 minutes

Ingredients

- Chopped raw veggie salad
- 1 orange pepper (minced) (about 1 cup)
- 1 yellow pepper (small cut) (about 1 cup)
- 5-8 radishes (halve and cut into thin slices) (about 3/4 cup)
- small head of broccoli (minced) (about 2 cups)
- 1 seedless cucumber (small cut) (about 2 cups)
- 1 cup of halved red seedless grapes
- 2-3 tablespoons chopped fresh dill
- 1/4 cup chopped fresh parsley
- 1/4 cup of raw peeled sunflower seeds
- 1/8 cup raw hemp hearts (peeled hemp seeds)
- Oil-free dressing
- garlic clove (chopped)
- tablespoons of red wine vinegar
- 1 tablespoon of apple cider vinegar
- Juice of 1 lemon
- 1 tbsp Dijonsenf
- 1 tbsp pure maple syrup
- 1/2 teaspoon salt (or to taste)
- 1/8 tsp pepper (or to taste)

Preparation

Whisk the ingredients - Chopped raw veggie salad, 1 orange pepper, yellow pepper, radishes, small head of broccoli, seedless cucumber, halved red seedless grapes, chopped fresh dill, chopped fresh parsley, raw peeled sunflower seeds, raw hemp hearts, garlic clove, red wine vinegar, apple cider vinegar, lemon, Dijonsenf, pure maple syrup, salt, pepper. For dressing inside a small bowl and set aside.

Combine all the salad ingredients in a large bowl.

Pour the dressing over the chopped vegetables then wrap well.

Cover and then refrigerate it for an hour or two and toss the salad once or twice during this time to coat evenly. Enjoy!

Notes on the recipe

The dimensions of the cut vegetables are estimates. It does not have to be accurate as long as it is close. If you want, you can swap the orange or yellow pepper for red. This recipe is quite versatile and could easily be doubled for a large amount.

Nutritional information

- Calories: 111
- Total Fat: 2g
- Saturated Fat: 1g
- Cholesterol: 10mg
- Sodium: 58mg
- Carbohydrates: 19g
- Sugar: 18 g
- Calcium: 15%

26.**Mediterranean Veggie Pita Sandwich**

Makes 2 pita bread, can be multiplied for more portions

Time preparation: 4hours: 30mins

Ingredients

- 1/4 cup chopped carrots
- A handful of baby spinach
- 1/4 cup chickpeas
- 1 tsp of crumbled feta cheese
- 2 tsp. of fine chopped sun-dried tomatoes

- 2 teaspoons of chopped kalamata olives
- Season with salt and pepper

Preparation

The chopped carrots, baby spinach, chickpeas, crumbled feta cheese, chopped sun-dried tomatoes, chopped kalamata olives, salt and pepper. Spread the bath in every pita pant. Sort the rest of the ingredients between the boxes. Eat immediately or pack in a container for lunch. Cool the device if you prepare it for more than 4 hours before eating.

Nutritional information

- Calories 287.6
- Sodium 716.0 mg
- Potassium 263.6 mg
- Total Carbohydrate 45.7 g
- Dietary Fiber 6.8 g

27.Pumpkin filled with vegetables and quinoa

Time preparation: 35 minutes

Ingredients

4 portions

- 2 pieces of Italian pumpkin
- 2 tablespoons olive oil
- 1 tablespoon of onion
- Cut 2 pieces of carrots into strips
- In Cut 1 piece of potato into cubes
- Cut 2 pieces of paprika into strips

- 1 cup of cooked quinoa
- 1 teaspoon curry
- Enough of ground bread
- To the taste of salt and pepper

Preparation

1. Preheat the oven to 180 ° C

2. Cut the Italian pumpkin lengthwise and remove the filling place with water in a bowl.

3. Heat over medium heat in a pan, add the oil, quinoa and onion, add the carrots, potatoes and paprika and cook for 3 minutes, season with salt and pepper curry.

4. Put the pumpkins in a tray and fill with the filling, place on the ground bread and bake for 10 minutes.

Nutritional information

- Percent of daily values based on a 2,000 calorie diet.
- calories 232 kcal 12%
- Carbohydrates 40.4 g 13%
- Proteins 8,9 g 18%
- Lipids 3.8 g 5.8%
- Fiber 4.4 g 8.9%
- sugar 0.2 g 0.2%

- Cholesterol 0.0 mg 0.0%

28.Quinoa confetti

Time preparation: 30 minutes

Ingredients

4 portions

- 1 1/2 cups vegetable stock (low sodium) or water
- 1 cup of well-washed and drained quinoa
- 1/2 teaspoon salt
- 1/2 teaspoon black pepper

- 1 cup of mixed frozen vegetables (e.g carrots, peas, corn, etc.)

Preparation

1. Add the vegetable stock or water in a medium saucepan over medium heat and bring everything to a boil.
2. Add quinoa, salt, and pepper, reduce to low heat and cover the pan with a lid. Cook it until the liquid has evaporated and the quinoa is soft for about 15 minutes. Remove the lid, pour in the vegetables and move it with a fork. Cover again so that the vegetables are cooked with the steam of quinoa.

Nutritional information

Percent of daily values based on a 2,000-calorie diet.

- Calories 268 kcal 13%
- Carbohydrates 45, 3 g 15%
- Proteins 11, 8 g 24%
- Lipids 4, 0 g 6, 1%
- Fiber 7, 4 g 15%
- Sugar 1.2 g 1.3%
- Cholesterol 0, 0 mg 0.0%

29.Shrimp and Zucchini Skewers

Time preparation: 25 minutes

Ingredients

- Zucchini
- Prawns
- Cold water

Preparation

As simple as alternating slices of zucchini rolled with prawns in the middle and roasting on a griddle a couple of minutes per side. So that the zucchini slices do not break when rolled, squeeze them a little first and then pass them through cold water.

Nutritional Information

- Calories 87
- Calories from Fat 13 % Daily Value
- Total Fat 2g2%
- Saturated Fat 1g2%
- Monounsaturated Fat 0g
- Polyunsaturated Fat 0g
- Cholesterol 0mg0%
- Sodium 30mg1%
- Total Carbohydrate 17g6%
- Dietary Fiber 5g22%
- Sugars 13g
- Protein 7g

30.Thai steak salad with herbs and onions

Time preparation: 25 minutes

Ingredients

For four portion

- One flank or rump steak (600 g)
- Salt
- 1 tbsp. peanut oil
- Two red onions
- 1 piece Ginger (20 g)
- One red chili pepper
- One cucumber

- 3 handful Asian herbs (30 g)
- 1 tbsp. rice vinegar
- 3 tbsps. lime juice
- 2 tbsps. Fish sauce
- 1 tsp. honey
- Paprika
- Chili powder
- Pepper
- meat

Preparation

1. Rinse meat, one flank or rump steak, pat dry and salt. Heat the peanut oil and then fry the steak on both sides for 6-8 minutes over high heat. Remove meat from the frying pan and let it rest.
2. Meanwhile, peel onions and ginger. Halve onions and cut into strips. Chop ginger. Cut chili pepper into half lengthwise remove seeds, wash and cut into fine rings. Clean the cucumber, wash, quarter it and slice it. Wash Asian herbs shake dry and peel off leaves.
3. Add ginger with vinegar, lime juice, fish sauce, honey and 2-3 tablespoons water to a dressing, season it with paprika, chili powder, salt, and pepper.

4. Slice the meat and arrange with herbs, chili rings, cucumber and onions on a plate and drizzle with the dressing.

Nutritional Information

Calories: 390 kcal

Intuitive Eating

1. Unconditional Permission to Eat (When Hungry and Desired Food): Unconditional permission to eat is defined as eating the desired food when the person feels physical hunger. Individuals who exhibit this type of eating behavior neither try to ignore their physical hunger nor tend to avoid eating unacceptable foods by classifying them as acceptable and unacceptable. Eating behavior of individuals who give them unconditional permission to eat is controlled by physical hunger and satiety signals. Therefore, individuals with such eating behavior do not experience excessive eating behavior.

On the other hand, according to the researches, when, how much and what nutrients put conditions on their food, the feeling of deprivation and the state of the mind is constantly engaged in food. The most striking research to measure the physiological and psychological effects of dietary restriction, in other words, conditional eating behavior, is the Minnesota Starvation Experiment. Keys, Brozek, Henschel, Mickelsen and Taylor (1950), in a study conducted with 36 men aged 22 to 33 years, limited the daily calorie intake of participants to 1560 kilocalories for 6 months. As a result of this strict diet program, it was found that the participants' minds were constantly busy with food and showed binge eating behavior when they stopped dieting.

In the study of Herman and Polivy (1988), it was observed that individuals restricting daily calorie intake exhibited excessive eating behavior as a result of breaking dietary rules or consuming foods that they call forbidden food. They tend to eat, and when they reach physical saturation, they stop eating. These individuals who show eating behavior based on their physical hunger use food as fuel. In contrast, individuals with impaired eating patterns, even though they do not feel physical hunger, they tend to eat to cope with the fluctuations in their mood, and even if they reach physical saturation, they do not stop eating until they reach emotional fullness. These individuals who display eating behavior based on their emotional hunger use food as a tool.

Physical hunger is felt in the lower part of the body and a few hours after eating. Emotional hunger is felt in the upper part of the body and independent of eating times. Physical hunger ends with the body's energy intake. However, emotional hunger, despite the feeling of satiety, ends up with more energy intake than the body needs. Although physical hunger is removed when a feeling of satisfaction occurs, when emotional hunger is relieved, feelings of guilt and embarrassment emerge. Physical Fasting and Toughness

The state of awareness is an innate ability. Birch, Johnson, Andresen, Petersen and Schulte (1991), when examining the eating behavior of children between 2 and 5 years of age, although the amount of food consumed by children varies at a meal, they found that there is no difference between the total amount of calories taken daily. Most caregivers observe the variability in children's eating behavior and conclude that they cannot adequately regulate food intake and adopt compelling strategies to control children's eating behavior. Such strategies are counterproductive, as they impose external rules instead of innate signals of innate hunger and saturation, and lead to a break from internal experience and innate ability to regulate food intake. Indeed, In children who were forced to eat, weight gain, tendency to eat without feeling physical hunger and eating behavior to cope with their emotions were observed. 8 In the study of Faith, Scanlon, Birch, Francis and Sherry (2004), it was found that children whose food intake was restricted by their parents showed eating behavior even though they did not feel physical hunger and body mass indices (BMI) were higher than children whose food intake was not restricted by their parents. It was found that. The philosophy underlying intuitive eating can be summarized as the individual's innate knowledge and awareness of supporting this type of eating, and all he has to do is rely on the physical signals coming from his body. Intuitive eating supports the principle of eating when the abdomen is hungry and stop eating when the abdomen is saturated.

10 Principles of Intuitive Eating

1. Reject Diet Mentality. Throw away diet books and magazines that give you false hopes of losing weight more quickly, easily and permanently. Take a stand against all these diet lies that make you feel unsuccessful when you start a new diet program, but you don't get results or you get all the weight back. If you have any hope of developing a new diet program that will work miracles, this will prevent you from exhibiting intuitive eating attitudes and behaviors.

2. Respect Your Feeling of Hunger. Get enough energy and eat carbohydrates to feed your body biologically. Otherwise, you can trigger over-eating behavior, which is the primitive impulse. When you reach the point of extreme hunger, you will be away from restrained and conscious eating behavior. However, if you respect the

feeling of hunger, the biological signal, you will see that your body eats as much as it needs. With this experience, you will regain your confidence in restrained meals.

3. Peace with Food. Declare a truce and put an end to your battle with food! Allow yourself to eat unconditionally. If you stipulate that you should not eat yourself a certain food; this attitude can lead to a feeling of deprivation, which can lead to craving and binge eating behavior that you cannot avoid.

4. Challenge the Food Police. Food Police controls the unreasonable rules created by the diet mindset. Therefore, you must challenge the Food Police, which calls you good for eating under 1000 calories but bad for eating a slice of chocolate cake. By removing Food Police from your life, you will have taken an important step towards regaining your intuitive eating ability.

5. Respect Your Feeling of Toughness. Listen to the body signals that you are no longer hungry. When you reach saturation, observe the symptoms that occur in your body. Take a break into the middle of your meal and question both the taste of the food you eat and the level of saturation you feel at that moment.

6. Discover the Satisfaction Factor. We sometimes ignore feelings of pleasure and satisfaction from the act of

eating, which is the most basic gift of our existence. Whereas, when you allow yourself to eat the food you desire at that moment, you will create a attractive and inviting environment for yourself. If you allow this experience, you will see that you have achieved the feeling that you have eaten enough by consuming less food than you anticipated.

7. Feel the Feeling Before You Tend to Eat. Find more effective ways to solve your problems, soothe yourself, feed emotionally, or distract yourself from food. Emotions such as anxiety, loneliness, boredom and anger are feelings that we all experience throughout our lives. Each emotion has its own triggering causes and coping methods. Food, numb our feelings you'll see that you've reached the feeling you've eaten enough, consuming less food than you anticipated.

Find more effective ways to solve your problems, soothe yourself, feed emotionally, or distract yourself from food. Emotions such as anxiety, loneliness, boredom and anger are feelings that we all experience throughout our lives. Each emotion has its own triggering causes and coping methods. Food, numb our feelings emotions that we all experience throughout our lives.

Rak or by distracting us from our pains, although it gives us a short-term feeling of comfort, it does not help solve the problems we face. In fact, it causes our problems to grow exponentially due to feelings of guilt resulting from excessive eating.

8. Respect Your Body. Accept your genetic structure. Just as a person with shoe size 38 does not have the expectation of entering shoe number 36, the same person should have the same expectation of size. Individuals who have been enslaved to dieting mentality want to have unrealistic body dimensions, so they show an extreme critical approach to their bodies. When you respect the body you have, you love and accept yourself.

9. Exercise - Feel the Difference. Be active and feel the difference. Change your focus: Instead of you concentrating on the calorie-burning effect of exercise, focus on how you move within your body during exercise. When your goal is to feel good instead of losing weight, you will be more motivated to exercise.

10. Respect Your Health; Tolerant Nutrition. Make your food choices considering your health and taste. You don't need to go through a unique diet to be healthy. A snack or a meal doesn't put you on weight, nor does it cause nutritional shortages. For a healthy diet, it is sufficient to

demonstrate consistent and stable eating attitudes and behaviors.

Research On Intuitive Eating Attitudes And Behaviors

Scientific research was needed to objectively examine intuitive eating attitudes and behaviors. In order to be used in these scientific studies, it was necessary to develop a scale that graded intuitive eating attitudes and behaviors. Realizing this need, Tracy Tylka developed the Intuitive Eating Scale (IES) in 2006, originally called the Intuitive Eating Scale (IES). When designing the scale, Tracy Tylka was based on the three basic elements mentioned above, developed by Tribole and Resch. In the scale consists of 21 items, Tylka and Kroon Van Diest developed the Intuitive Eating Scale-2 (IES-2) scale. This new scale consists of 23 items; 11 original and 12 new items. The IES-2 scale, unconditional permission to eat, eating based on physical rather than emotional causes, There are 4 sub-tests: relying on physical hunger and satiety symptoms and body-food selection compliance when deciding when and how much to eat. Increasing scores indicate an increase in the tendency to show intuitive eating attitudes and behaviors.

The first study of intuitive eating and attitude behavior was conducted in 2006 by Tylka, who developed the IES scale. In this study, individuals with intuitive eating attitudes and behaviors were found to have high self-esteem and low BMI. It was also found that these individuals were more optimistic and did not tend to internalize the thin body ideal created by contemporary culture. 2 As the result of the research conducted by Madden, Leong, Gray and Horwath (2012); they had low BMI and a 10-point increase in the scale corresponded to a 4.5 kilogram decrease in total weight. Gast, Nielsen, Hunt, and Leiker (2015) found that women with high scores on the IES scale had low BMI and that these women had internal motivation to exercise. August-Horvath and Tylka (2011) found that the acceptance of their bodies by others has a predictive effect on women's appreciation of their bodies and their intuitive eating behavior. Dockendorff, Petrie, Greenlef, and Martin (2012) adapted the IES scale to adolescents and as a result of the study, it was determined that adolescents exhibiting intuitive eating behavior did not tend to internalize low BMI, positive mood and thin body ideal. As a result of Galloway, Farrow and Martz (2010), it was found that university students who had parents who control eating behavior and restrict eating in childhood had higher BMI, exhibited emotional eating behavior and had low scores on IES scale compared to other students. Hawks, Madanat, Hawks and Harris (2005), when examining the effect of intuitive eating on physical health, found that women with intuitive eating behavior, serum triglyceride levels were significantly lower. As a result of this research, it is claimed that intuitive eating behavior has a predictive effect on decreasing the risk of heart diseases.

In summary, in the researches, intuitive eating attitudes and behaviors and body image, physical awareness level, a positive correlation was found between self-perception and life satisfaction levels, however, with intuitive eating attitudes and behaviors.

A negative correlation was found between the tendency to internalize the slim body ideal, BMI and eating disorder symptoms. Considering the results of the studies, it has become important to develop intervention techniques to gain intuitive eating skills in order to increase the effectiveness of eating disorder treatment.

This Is The Danger Of Mindless Eating (And 6 Tips To Eat More Mindful)

Living consciously can be done in many different ways. In this way you can make conscious choices about what you do today, who you see, how much time you spend with it, where you shop and what clothing you wear. But you can also consciously do all these activities again, and that has more advantages than you might think. That is why we are talking about mindful food today.

Mindful food may sound floating, but it is anything but. It is perhaps even one of the best diets that exist. We explain how that works.

Research shows that the average American eats about 2.5 hours a day. Half of that time we are happily doing something else. Talking, scrolling over your Instagram, reading the newspaper or whatever: at least not just eating alone. And if we do that anyway, it is often a bite to eat.

We are constantly looking for distraction. But why? You will miss the taste sensations, the smell, the texture and the pleasure of eating. I say, a loyal supporter of the bite-swallow-away method. I know, but I still find it difficult: mindful food.

Mindful eating is focusing on the food that you are eating. From the products that you choose in the store to how you ultimately pimp it up. Mindfulness is being present in the moment, and in this case that is at the table.

The danger of mindless eating

Nutritionist and teacher at Harvard Medical School, Lillian Cheung, calls this behavior mindless food. According to her, it could even be the reason that there are as many health problems as obesity in America. "It's probably linked to the lack of knowledge and awareness about the food we consume." Quite confronting.

This research shows that mindful eating could help with weight problems, staying away from processed foods and even making healthier choices in the supermarket. This is not about counting calories, fats or carbohydrates, but about adjusting your mindset. A lot easier than many a yo-yo diet.

Tip to eat more mindful

We therefore share some practical tips from Treehugger that help you eat more mindfully:

Eat if you are hungry (don't wait until you're hungry)

Okay in the Netherlands we are never really hungry, but at least don't eat until your stomach rattles. Preferably eat before your appetite starts to get worse. In this way you prevent eating everything within two bites to satisfy the feeling of hunger as quickly as possible. It may take a while, but practice makes perfect.

Have you ever heard of the various forms of hunger? Try to know the difference between physical and emotional hunger. Sweets at work probably have more to do with boredom than you really need food. Do you want to nibble something? Then make one of these healthy snacks.

Avoid distractions while eating

You can do mindful eating together and you don't have to be quiet on your own. But focus on what's on your plate. We bet that you will taste the flavors much more intensely if you pay more attention to them.

Eat slowly

However difficult this may be for some people, eating slowly is a must with conscious eating. Not only because you enjoy more, you chew more and eat less until you are full. Conversely, even fast eating is linked to being overweight, because it feels like you are not yet full and bragging even more so that you end up far too full.

It only takes about 20 minutes for your body to notice that you have had enough. Are you still hungry afterwards? Then you know for sure that you are still hungry.

Enjoy with all your senses

If you don't have a distraction, your senses will automatically turn on. Your food contains more than just taste. You can also enjoy the texture, the smell, the colors and what it looks like. Take your time and you are guaranteed to enjoy your plate of food more than when you almost breathe it in for the TV.

Stop. with. food. as. you. full. sit.

Enough is enough. Fast eaters might find out a bit later, but it is really discouraged. As you may have noticed, a lot of food is tasty at the moment itself, but it becomes rather unpleasant after a minute or so. In addition, overeating (binge eating) is generally not particularly good for your body either. Conversely, eating slowly helps you feel when you are full, so that you do not eat too much.

Do your shopping consciously

If you want to eat (more) consciously, it actually starts in the supermarket. Be aware of the products that you put in your basket and that you will eat later. Preferably buy healthy, sustainably sourced and organic products. These ultimately contribute to a healthy and happy you.

Free from guilt in our relationship with food

It is very possible that if you are struggling with weight and the way you eat, you may feel guilty about not being able to win that battle. Maybe if you understand that we are a species that for two million years we have been programmed to see food and eat because our bodies and brains developed to live in times of shortage and that we are adapted to store excess energy maybe you can put this feeling of guilt under the focus of compassion and kindness.

It is important to be able to broaden our perspective and develop compassion towards the complexity of our relationship with food, our way of eating and our body weight. If we stop blaming ourselves on our eating behavior and our weight, maybe we can connect with our vulnerability and shame and develop a broader perspective to find a more balanced vision and perception. Many diets contain the hidden message that having a problem with weight means that something is wrong with our person. Tara Brach speaks of the "trance of lack of worth" as a situation in which we are afraid of being defective and that is accompanied by a feeling of separation from others and life.

Alongside this fear, a reaction usually arises that is usually blaming or even feeling hate for what we consider the cause of the problem: ourselves, other people or life itself.

Thus self-recrimination, guilt and self-hate lead us to an added suffering many times of all unnecessary. These emotions and feelings can lead us to try to escape from suffering by entering into addictions such as overeating, drinking alcohol, drugs or engaging in love relationships and codependency in which we have to receive the value from abroad. This lack of worth may even cause us a distrust and doubt that others may love us because, deep down, we fear that at some point they will realize our lack of worth and reject us.

This lack of worth and imperfection, never allows us to relax and whatever happens we are always looking for defects in ourselves that do not allow us to relax and enjoy the adventure of life. Thus, self-criticism, in addition to disconnecting ourselves, becomes a way of protecting us from the idea that others can harm us, because we are already prepared with the "protection" of our own criticism.

Usually the fierce criticism ends up producing a feeling of chronic guilt and rejection of ourselves. Dislike can be presented in two ways, one very energetic and overflowing as anger and hate, but also another very subtle and contained as grief, fear, disappointment and despair. This form of aversion is an energy that freezes and paralyzes and usually manifests itself as guilt.

Guilt engages in an internal dialogue of thoughts such as "I am the most horrible person in the world, I am the only one who commits such horrible acts" that deep down are a magnification of the ego. The Buddha in observing his own suffering made a wonderful discovery and it was that all suffering comes from the erroneous notion that we are a separate and separate self. This idea of the ego has us imprisoned in continuous cycles of desire and aversion.

Desire - clinging, greed, attachment - is a state of mind that defines what we think we need to be happy. We project all our dreams and hopes of realizing ourselves in getting some object that demands our attention. This can be a certain activity, a result, a specific thing or person. Deceived by our fleeting illusion, we contemplate the world with tunnel vision. If we let ourselves be dragged by desire, we stand firmly in the linear time frame. We focus on getting what we don't have yet or keeping what we have. We are oriented towards the future. Caught up by this concept of linear time, we end up in what the Buddhist teachings call bhava, or become, always rush into the next moment. It is as if before each breath ends we lean forward to inhale again. In this way the ego, through desire, confines us in one of those cycles that lead us to suffering by taking us out of the present moment.

What we know as the "I" is an aggregate of thoughts, emotions and patterns of family behaviors. The mind combines them with each other, forging a story about a personal, individual entity, with continuity over time and that has a fixed character. Both fear and desire are natural energies, which are part of nature's designs and that serve to protect us and move forward. But when guilt, fear and desire become the very core of our identity, we lose sight of the fullness of our being.

In order to overcome guilt, ego, anger or hate, the practice of meditation can lead us to notice the impersonal nature of reality; of the forces, energies and thoughts that arise and disappear, and we can begin to experience a very different reality. We can see anger, guilt or grief emerging in the mind as forces that come and go. Dislike is like a summer storm that comes and goes. When we begin to see that impermanence, insubstantiality and suffering are characteristics of the reality we live in, we can release that feeling that there is something wrong with us. It is more when we observe other beings and ourselves when metta or unconditional love begins to emerge.

Guilt can be considered as a manifestation of anger or hate. The Buddha said that hate can never be extinguished by hate, only the cessation of hate can be achieved by love. If we apply this maxim to guilt, forgiveness is what can allow us to recover a part of ourselves that has been enslaved by an event of the past.

To get rid of a deep aversion to oneself and others we must be able to practice forgiveness. He has the power to ripen the forces of purity like those of love, and to affirm the qualities of patience and compassion. Create the space for renewal and a life free from the servitude of the past.

When you are a prisoner of your past actions or the actions of another, you are not able to fully live your present existence. Resentment, partly experienced pain and the ungrateful inheritance of the past come together to close your heart and, consequently, reduce your world.

The intention of the meditation of forgiveness is not to force something or pretend or forget yourself in excessive deference to the needs of others. In fact, thanks to the great compassion for you, you create the conditions of a love without hindrance, which can end the separation and relieve you of the two twin charges of lacerating guilt and perpetually unresolved outrage.

Giving is an integral part of forgiveness. When you give, you make an offering to ourselves and others, creating a willingness to make peace with the conflict and pain that feed our anger, resentment and bitterness.

It may be easier to be critical of us and say "I hate my body" for being like that, or not forgetting that person hurt me. But when we act like this, we are really clinging, as the Buddha said to a burning coal that whoever burns first is my own person.

It is much harder to forgive than not to forgive. It is not easy to access that place within you, capable of forgiving and loving.

Forgiveness begins with an intention of wanting to let go, of observing our tendency to stick to hate. By forgiving we create a space to establish skillful habits and mental states that are in harmony with the desire to change. Forgiveness also lessens the stress that comes from judging ourselves and others.

Forgiveness does not mean condoning a harmful action or denying injustice and suffering. Never be confused with passivity in the face of rape or abuse. Forgiveness is an intimate renunciation of guilt or resentment.

Initially we can start by forgiving ourselves: your mistakes, feelings and the habits. From this perspective, it is seen that everything is equally forgivable, whether it is our laziness, hatred of my person, impatience, like big thighs, or the tendency to overeat.

The will to be aware of what is being asked for forgiveness is a perspective and a radical step already in themselves. For this it may be useful to make a list of the things we find difficult to forgive.

For this you can practice the following exercise for a while. For this I invite you to sit in a quiet and comfortable place, in a relaxed posture.

Repeat the phrases on your list starting with small things like "not getting enough exercise" and ending with bigger issues like "the habit of mistreating myself for not being a perfect person."

Mentally repeat phrases such as:

To the extent that I am much capable, I forgive myself for any damage or harm that I have caused myself with or without intention.

To the extent that I am capable able, I forgive myself for not getting adequate exercise. Even if I cannot forgive myself, I forgive myself for this.

Me .... (placing your own name in the ellipses) I forgive myself for ... (the action or the reason you presented on the list)

Me .... (placing your own name in the ellipses) I forgive myself for all the ways in which I have been harmed, aggrieved, knowingly or without noticing.

For as long as necessary, I will make the effort to offer myself the invaluable gift of forgiveness.

It is useful to do the practice of forgiveness every day, including any aspect of yourself or your experience that can benefit from this practice.

Next, we focus on forgiving others. Once again, we start with small problems and continue with the biggest ones (if necessary maybe you can make another list).

Mentally repeat phrases like:

To the extent that I am capable, I forgive my friend Lucia for the damage or injury I have experienced. Even if I can't forgive her totally, I forgive myself for that.

Me .... (placing your own name in the ellipses) I forgive you ... (placing the name of the person you forgive in the ellipses)

For as long as necessary, I will make the effort to offer Lucia the invaluable gift of forgiveness.

Finally we apologize to others.

Mentally repeat phrases like:

To the extent that I am capable, if I have harmed someone, knowingly or without noticing I ask for your forgiveness.

Allow this request to warm up inside you and if a heaviness arises, images or evoke memories or actions, free yourself from the burden and mentally exclaim: I apologize.

For as long as necessary, I will make the effort to apologize.

During this practice, many contradictory emotions may emerge: shame, anger, pain for the damage caused, the impression of being betrayed, confusion or doubt. Try to let these states arise without judging them. Recognize them as natural facts and then calmly turn your attention to the exercise of forgiveness.

With habitual practice, we begin to realize that forgiveness is a unique way of feeding, a way of providing ourselves and others a space around our conflicts and difficulties. We no longer feel so alone, isolated, or doomed to failure. The peace that arises in the mind provides an inner fullness that no amount of food can ever offer.

How Do We Explain Children What Is The Minfulness?

Open observation, curious and without prior judgment is an art that children understand perfectly. As we become adults, doubts and preconceived opinions arrive. The truth is that children are artists of attention in the here and now, they live in the present.. It is easy to observe for example when you see a child with an adult waiting at a bus stop. The child is likely to use this present tense to enjoy the fallen leaves in the fall or to try to find balance with his body somewhere in the street. While the adult at this time it is easy to see him with his eyes lost in the worries of day to day (the shopping list, the work schedule ...) or worse, lost on the screen of a mobile phone with some entertainment.

It is clear that we can learn a lot from children about mindfulness but ... how do we make them aware of the benefits of this practice? Because most likely, if they do not practice it habitually, eventually becoming adults, they gradually fell into the adult stress of living in the worries of the past or the fears of the future.

The Globe Game

This game is done in large groups, all sitting in a circle with a balloon previously decorated with beautiful pictures and words.

In the beginning, we tell the children that we are going to pass the globe from hand to hand AS FAST AS THEY CAN.

This round is as you can imagine very funny and full of contagious laughter of children.

Then we ask them to pass the globe from hand to hand but THE MOST SLOWLY THEY CAN, as if they were in space without gravity. In the first round we ask you to look at the characteristics of the globe, in the details that you could not see before: color, texture, drawings and written words ... In a second round, we invite you to pass the globe and smile at the companion at looking into his eyes. This moment is magical!

MINDFULNESS

After this activity, children understand the need to train our mind to be more attentive, more aware. We all want a mind capable of capturing all the details and we know that MINDFULNESS is the best tool!!

INITIAL GREETING

To train our mind and be AWARE AND AWARE we must learn to sit and remain in the POSTURE OF THE MIND ATTENTION (mindfull posture) The YOGAMUSIC song is a marabillous tool. Look how well we do it!!

How Unhealthy Are Industrial Foods Really?

Those who doesn't eat a lot of homemade food and eat a lot of industrial food increase their risk of getting fat and sick. Nevertheless, highly processed foods also have advantages: they create above all women's freedoms.

Although currently circulating all sorts of more or less healthy diets. But no matter if it's low-carb, stone-age food or clean eating, all of you have shot at an enemy: highly processed food. The best way to avoid it completely, or at least eat only very rarely. Even the German Society for Nutrition (DGE) recommends that one should choose as fresh as possible foods for his health and consume finished products only occasionally. But are the so-called convenience products, which make our everyday life easier, really unhealthy? To approach the subject scientifically , Carlos Monteiro, a health scientist at the University of Sao Paulo in 2010, provided a definition. The so-called "NOVA food classification" divides food into four groups.

Recently, Monteiro has presented a revised versionIn the first group, the unprocessed or poorly processed products, such as fresh fruits and vegetables, as well as meat, fish, eggs or milk, gather. Even dried fruit and frozen vegetables or fish are considered less processed. Group 2 contains oil, flour, salt and sugar. Group 3 comprises the processed products cheese, bread, ham, noodles, but also canned tomatoes or smoked fish. These products are usually ready to eat, but contain only two or three ingredients. Group 4 now contains the proscribed "ultra-processed" foods. They have gone through several stages of processing, supplying a whole range of ingredients and additives that are not easily recognizable as food. This category includes soft drinks, sweets, meat products, bakery products,

Claudia and Almut, nutritionists at the University of Paderborn, have adapted the NOVA list to German practices and grouped the food consumed here into three groups: fresh, processed and highly processed foods. With this tool in hand, in 2015, the researchers examined how the consumption of highly processed foods affects the health of children and adults.

The more finished products, the more overweight

The result is clear: the more finished products on the menu, the more overweight people are. The researchers explain this with the fact that foods such as French fries, frozen pizza or chocolate have a comparatively high energy density, in other words provide many calories. And these calories come mainly from sugar, white flour and fat, mostly from saturated fat and partly from trans fatty acids. But these products provide less protein or fiber. Both food ingredients, however, saturate what prevents overweight.

Also, people who eat many high-processed products were less well supplied with calcium and folate, an important B-vitamin. For this they took more saline. In children, such a diet resulted in a 17 percent higher intake of sodium than in fresh food. Salt is considered to be the cause of hypertension - and appetite stimulants. Of course, a ready meal can also have a good quality. Nevertheless, the entirety of what is being prepared in the industrial kitchen seems to be rather unfavorable.

Such a mixture of bad fat, sugar and salt meanwhile hold many scientists regardless of the high energy content of food for the cause of the overweight epidemic. Because these substances trigger reward systems in our brains while obstructing satiety mechanisms, as has been shown countless studies with animals and humans. David Kessler is a physician and former head of the US Food and Drug Administration, writes in his book The End of the Big Food: "Highly processed foods are changing the connections between the neural circuits in the brain and their patterns of reaction, with the result that we always want more of it."The easy availability of such products, at every gas station, every kiosk or bakery, exacerbates the problem.

Interaction of the ingredients makes the difference

However, the industry never tires of claiming that the ingredients they use are also found in natural foods and therefore pose no threat. »However, it is becoming increasingly clear that the so-called matrix of a food is partly responsible for its digestibility and its effect in the body, says Monteiro. The term "matrix" refers to the interaction of different ingredients that interact chemically and physically.

An example: An apple contains a lot of fructose (fructose), which has become disreputable in large quantities as liver damage. However, fiber such as pectins, which are stuck in the cell walls, prevents the sugar from entering the bloodstream too quickly. The blood sugar levels and the hormones involved are thus less strained than when you consume the same amount of fructose in the form of apple juice, in which the sugar is already dissolved and occurs without the pectin. On the other hand, saturated fatty acids applyas heartbreaking, in milk, however, they could even be healthy. In addition, highly processed foods just do not provide the same ingredients as fresh foods. "They also lack secondary phytochemicals, which are said to have many beneficial health effects," says Monteiro.

That could explain why industrial food not only thickens but also has other harmful effects. A recent study by the Universidad Navarra with almost 15,000 healthy participants shows that after nine years, people who indulged in the "cafeteria diet" had a higher risk of developing high blood pressure than fresh food fans. In addition, the sugar metabolism gets mixed up with a lot of industrial food in the long term, which promotes the development of diabetes.

Alienation of fresh food

Ultimately, the many additives are seen critically. Although their use must be safe for health. However, children who consume large amounts of sweets, flavored drinks or breakfast cereals sometimes exceed the limits of some dyes . "In addition, the use of preservatives, colorants and flavor enhancers is leading to an ever greater distance from the fresh, unprocessed product," says Niggemeier. Who eats such products often trimms his taste so strong stimuli, which means that fresh food tastes not so good.

On top of that, the finished products do not provide variety, and that is the top priority of healthy nutrition. Although the multicolored packaging suggests a wealth of variants, the majority of supermarket products contain cheap raw materials such as wheat, milk, sugar or palm oil. According to a report from the Austrian Ministry of Health in 2015 , about 30 percent of supermarket products contain wheat fractions. For example, ingredients such as gluten in industrial bread are present in higher quantities than in the sourdough bread from the baker next door - this can cause problems for the digestive machinery, which is calibrated for complexity.

Working women cook less and live more unhealthily

One thing is for sure: Highly processed foods should not be used too often. However, the actual consumption goes away from the fresh, home-cooked meal to finished product and fast food. According to the Federal Ministry of Food and Agriculture, 55 per cent of Germans said that easy and quick preparation was an important criterion in food purchasing in 2016, compared with just 45 per cent in 2015. At the time, 37 percent cooked twice or three times a week, compared to just 33 percent in 2016. Around 11 percent of Germans never use a cooking spoon, and women cook more often, but less often with work.

Of course, even a home-cooked meal can have miserable quality. Nevertheless, the liveliness increases the likelihood of a healthy overall diet. For example, women who cook almost every day eat more than twice as many vegetables as the cooking muffle. They consume ten times less snacks and only about 60 percent of the amount of sweetened beverages compared to women who never cook.

However, sociologists warn that one should not demonize the industrial products. "A relaxed approach to industrial food is by no means the downfall of food culture in Germany," says Daniel Kofahl, nutrition sociologist at the Office for Agricultural Policy and Food Culture. "For women and mothers in particular, this means a lot of relief in a hectic time when they have unnecessarily put pressure on culinary entitlement thinking in Germany for a long time." Mothers who do not stand by the stove every day have more time for the children, for sports or to read a good book. "When it comes to food choices, health is not per se and always the more valuable asset," says Petra Kolip, a health scientist at the University of Bielefeld.

In addition, some companies are now trying to improve their recipes; "reformulation" is the magic word. So far, however, this is voluntary, and consumers are not quite happy, because reformulated products are often associated with costs and a higher price. It is also unclear whether the new recipes are so much better then. There are currently doubts about sweeteners such as aspartame and sucralose, which are added to light drinks. They could not clearly prove in studies that they reduce the weight, but in some cases even the heart health worsened with high light drinks consumption.

In any case, cooking muffle can do some tricks: "If you combine finished products with vegetables and fruits, then this can also be a balanced meal," says Helmut Oberritter, CEO of DGE. Likewise, cooking does not have to be time-consuming: "We have a variety of good and fresh food as well as simple recipes at our disposal so that we can bring a healthy meal to the table in a short time," says Oberritter.

Why A Balanced Diet Is Your Key To Success

Far too often one hears beginners in the gym complain that they could eat now, since their diet has been changed, nothing more. This often ends in simplicity with a classic bodybuilder diet of rice and turkey. Of course you will not be able to live with this in the long run and live happily.

You will learn how to balance your diet so as not to lose the fun of eating. This will make it easier for you to change permanently.

Versatility Makes The Difference

Since at the end of the day only the calories and the macronutrient distribution play a decisive role in the diet, there are many foods that lead to the desired goal. You should, however, pay attention to what macronutrients you take, because carbohydrates are not equal to carbohydrates!

It is also vital for our health to look for a varied, varied and balanced diet. Only in this way is the absorption of all substances necessary for the body ensured.

The Length Matters!

As mentioned earlier, carbohydrates are not equal to carbohydrates. As every child knows, both simple sugars and starches are "saccharides". However, they have various effects on the body.

Our body can only use sugar in the form of glucose, that is, simple sugars. Since starch consists of many glucose molecules, it must first be "decomposed" by the body. This process takes time, which is why glucose is released successively.

If we eat high-glucose foods, the simple sugar in the blood rises very quickly and heavily because nothing has to be processed. due to the fact that starchy foods provide energy for a long time and glucose-containing foods only for a short time.

As a result, you should eat short-chain carbohydrates before and after training , and otherwise long-chain ones.

Good sources:

Short chain carbohydrates:

honey

Fruit (bananas etc)

Energy bar

Dark chocolate

Long-chain carbohydrates:

Sweet potatoes or potatoes

rice

noodles

Beans, peas etc.

Whole grain bread

Do Not Be Afraid Of Fats!

Like carbohydrates, many lay people are afraid of fats. This fear is of course unfounded and relies on many myths. In fact, fats are an essential building material of our body.

Fats, for example, play a decisive role in the transmission of stimuli and regulate our hormone balance. Every athlete knows how important the hormone balance is for muscle building and athletic success. Therefore, it can have fatal consequences to avoid fats in principle.

As with carbohydrates you have to differentiate with the fats. One differentiates in between saturated and unsaturated fatty acids. Often the saturated fatty acids are considered the "bad guys". But what is actually there?

Saturated fatty acids lead to heart attack?

There are several studies showing that saturated fat increases cholesterol and causes heart attacks. Again and again, however, new studies question exactly this. The statement that saturated fatty acids are unhealthy cannot therefore be supported on a flat-rate basis.

If you have a micronutrient-rich diet and enough exercise, you do not have to worry about saturated fat as part of your calorie balance.

Monounsaturated fatty acids

The monounsaturated fatty acids are not a problem for your health as part of a balanced diet. Like all other fats, they serve as an energy source.

One finds the monounsaturated fatty acids, for example in olive oil. The problem is only the trans fats, these are very common in industrial hardened fats. These should be avoided at all costs and should not be consumed too often as they can be problematic for our health.

Polyunsaturated fatty acids / essential fatty acids

Essential fatty acids belong to the group that your body can not produce itself. So he depends on you feeding her from outside.

The essential fatty acids are among the unsaturated fatty acids. One distinguishes between:

Omega 3

Omega 6

A good source of omega 3 is greasy fish, such as herring, tuna or salmon.

Vegan sources are linseed oil, hemp oil, walnut oil. These oils should not be utilized for cooking and should therefore be used only cold. In addition, chia seeds are a good omega 3 source and are also beneficial for our gut health.

Most of the time, Omega 6 is absorbed enough by the daily diet. It therefore makes sense to supplement Omega 3 to prevent an imbalance. Ideally, the ratio of Omega 6 to Omega 3 should be between 1: 1 and 5: 1.

Preparation Of Meals

Anyone who thinks it is enough to prepare their meals fresh is unfortunately mistaken. The proper preparation of meals is at least as important as the quality of the cooked foods. The reason for this is that by careful preparation important minerals and vitamins are preserved in the food.

But how do you optimally prepare your meals and what should be considered?

There are three principles that are important for the careful preparation of food:

low temperature

cook only for a short time

use as little fat as possible

These principles are important because otherwise you may lose important minerals and vitamins. This means that they are destroyed, for example, at too high temperatures. But even steaming at low temperatures can destroy vitamins if you kill the vegetables.

That you should use little fat for preparation should actually be known to athletes. By "little" is meant that the foods do not have to float in fat.

When using fat for searing, we recommend coconut oil because it offers a lot of health benefits. Pay attention to the additional "native" when buying. This stands for a cold-pressed and natural coconut oil. You should also make sure that it is oil and not coconut oil. Coconut oil is of inferior quality and is very heavily processed industrially.

How Often Should I Eat?

Many ask themselves this question. However, the question is not easy to answer. In the following we try to give you an idea why this is the case.

A role plays among other things:

personal circumstances (working, student, student, ...)

Habits

training frequency

training time

The personal circumstances are very individual. Someone who works and, for example, does an office job probably has more room to eat in between. However, someone who works on the job site and has regular breaks cannot eat 6 meals a day.

Another point to keep in mind when it comes to meal frequency is habits. Some people find it easier to eat three really big meals a day, not six small ones. The personal preferences are very different. What habits do you take care of?

The training frequency and exercise time also play a role. The reason for this is that our body is digesting after a meal and performance is reduced. That's why we should give our body a few hours after a meal to start the important digestive processes. In our opinion, three hours between meal and workout are optimal.

The balanced diet helped you and you realized that a well-balanced diet makes sense in sports activities. We benefit in many ways from the increased energy that we draw from real and natural food.

Low-processed foods simply bring us tremendous benefits, as they provide us with important micronutrients in addition to macronutrients. These are very important for us athletes because our body is constantly exposed to heavy loads and these nutrients, for example, for cell renewal and muscle building needed.

But not only the processing of the food must be considered, also the careful preparation of the freshest and least processed food you should make yourself the standard.

Overall, you should make sure that your diet is full, so you provide your body with enough liquid and energy from food available. However, the full nutrition is also characterized by the fact that vitamins, minerals, fiber and phytochemicals are covered in sufficient quantities by the diet.

What Does Science Say About The Diet Trend?

Many make the low carb diet, few know how it works. The body proves in artificial hunger metabolism how adaptable it is. But is that healthy?

1. What is a low carb diet?

Ketogenic diet, Atkins diet, New York diet - the low-carb diet has many names, all of which stand for the same principle: you eat less carbohydrates and more fat and protein. So carbohydrate-rich foods such as pasta, potatoes, bread and rice are removed from the diet and replaced with meals rich in fat and protein. A low-carb diet can be carried out with varying degrees of severity: The popular Atkins diet uses a maximum of 20 grams of carbohydrates per day, other approaches allow 50 to 100 grams. Thus, according to a plethora of dietary supplements, obese people can lose weight quickly and permanently.

2. How does a low carb diet work?

The goal of a low carb diet is to force the body to burn fat and melt hip gold. If you do without carbohydrates for a long time, the body switches from normal metabolism to an "artificial change of hunger". At this stage, the body responds as if it has been suffering from food deprivation for a long time - and attacks the fat reserves on the hip, stomach and buttocks. So that the body can use the fat as an energy source, it converts it into ketone bodies. These give their name to the ketogenic diet. Through the metabolism, the lack of carbohydrates can be almost completely compensated. Such a drastic reorganization of metabolism is an example of how adaptive our body is.

3. What happens at the biochemical level in the body during a low carb diet?

Normally, one lunch includes all three macronutrients: carbohydrates from pasta or potatoes; Fat made from cheese; Proteins from egg, fish or meat. All three substances are broken down in the course of their own metabolism into their basic components: In glycolysis, carbohydrates dissolve, the beta-oxidation breaks down fats, and the protein metabolism splits the proteins into amino acids.

Especially fast we can disassemble carbohydrates - in glucose, colloquially called grape sugar. Glucose is either further processed in glycolysis or it fills up the glycogen stores. This memory can empty the body during strenuous exercise and so quickly use the stored energy. In the long term, excess carbohydrates can be created as an energy reserve in the form of fat deposits. These processes are interrupted - due to lack of carbohydrates - during a low-carb diet; So the body has to resort to other sources of energy.

The energy is first provided by the high-fat and high-protein diet of the diet: The fat is broken down into its individual fatty acids or, just like the carbohydrates, stored in our fat cells for later. Proteins are not stored for the long term.

Although the metabolic pathways of the three macronutrients can be described separately, they are linked together: through the acetyl-CoA - the linchpin of our diet. The trick is that acetyl-CoA can come from any of the three metabolic pathways. Through this link, the body is able to compensate for the failure of the carbohydrate process.

Acetyl-CoA is also the key player during the ketogenic diet. If a human consumes little or no carbohydrates over a period of time, the body makes use of a trick in the first three to four days: it simply produces the missing glucose itself, from amino acids, the building blocks of the proteins that are produced during one Low-carb diet yes allowed to eat. But this trick, the so-called gluconeogenesis, is not enough to cover the energy needs. So the body taps into the next big energy storage: the dietary fat and the adipose tissue - the big goal of any diet.

The stored fat is thus dissolved again: This "fat burning", among other things glycerol is produced, which is rebuilt until it can hook into the cycle of glycolysis and thus replace the glucose. In other words, the carbohydrate metabolism continues to work partially without having to eat carbohydrates. As far as the theory, which is quite conclusive, but in practice holds some traps.

4. What roles do the ketone bodies play?

After several days of strict low-carbohydrate diets, the body completely switches to the hunger metabolism: it produces ketone bodies that can be used by the organs and especially the central nervous system as an energy source - as a substitute for the missing glucose.

Although ketone bodies can serve as replacement energy sources, their production is actually a reaction to excess acetyl-CoA. By burning fat too much of the substance is produced. But the body cannot metabolize such an amount of acetyl-CoA. Therefore, it accumulates in the liver. As a way out the body forms the ketone bodies, it is in the "ketogenesis".

5. What role does insulin play?

Most chemical processes in the body are controlled by hormones. Also in the dissolution of adipose tissue helps a hormone: the glucagon, the "antagonist" of insulin. Insulin is released when we eat carbohydrates. It ensures that the glucose is quickly incorporated into the glycogen storage or fat storage. Without carbohydrates in the diet, insulin levels remain low. As a result, the glucagon can promote the removal of fat deposits undisturbed.

6. Is it easy to lose weight with low-carb and without the yo-yo effect?

According to the current study situation, those who want to lose weight with a low-carbohydrate diet can lose a lot of weight during the first six months. Most nutritional studies draw a comparison between the two most popular diet forms: low-carb diet versus low-fat diet. Subjects declined more with low-carb than with low-fat. However, most of the lost kilos is probably due to excreted water, because the water loss is higher in a low-carb diet than other forms of diet.

In almost all nutritional studies, a striking pattern is repeated: Through a low-carb diet, the subjects decreased more and faster, but almost never long-term. Most of the studies were conducted for only six months and therefore too short to determine whether the success of the diet is permanent. The long-term studies show that the participants increase again on time from the sixth month, which may also be due to the fact that the subjects no longer strictly follow the study instructions after some time. But not only the low carb diet fails in the long run. In other diets, the yo-yo effect also beats after about six months.

Also a large overview study from the year 2014concludes that the achievements of a low carb diet only last for a short time. Instead, the scientists recommend that they feed only ketologically in phases. Their concept begins with 20 days of low-carbohydrate diet to achieve the hunger metabolism - ketogenesis. The following 20 days serve as a stabilization phase, in which the diet-willing, although only a little carbohydrates to eat, but should not remain in the ketogenesis. The subsequent four months are fed according to the Mediterranean diet, followed by another 20 days of low-carb diet. So a yo-yo effect can be avoided. However, in particular, transitions between diets should be slow and controlled, preferably under the supervision of a physician.

7. Is the low carb diet healthy?

So far, science has not provided a good answer to this question - there are no time-consuming studies investigating the actual long-term effects of a low-carbohydrate diet.

But there are all the more pseudo-scientific dietetters, in which especially one rule is constantly ruminated: For a successful acceptance of the obese should in principle simply take less kilocalories , as he consumed - no matter what is eaten. However, the macronutrient distribution (in whatever ratio) does not say anything about food quality, physiological effects in the body or health prognosis. Those who consume only red meat, eggs and artificial protein shakes within a low-carbohydrate diet are certainly not healthy. However, a low-carbohydrate diet can also consist of lots of green vegetables, beans and legumes, fish and dairy products. It depends mainly on the biological value That is, the question of how much body protein is produced from the amount of protein taken up.

A high-protein low-carb diet could also be dangerous to the heart. In particular, LDL cholesterol is considered one of the biggest risk factors for heart disease; but that too is being discussed). A meta-study from 2006 sees an increased risk for the increase in LDL concentration in a low-carb diet. Therefore, the desired results of a high-protein diet should be carefully weighed against this result.

A more recent long-term study published in 2012 warns of the risks of a low-carbohydrate diet. For 15 years, eating habits and diseases were documented by 43 396 Swedes. According to the authors, there is a direct link between a low carb high protein diet and the risk of cardiovascular disease. Other studies are investigating the influence of a high-protein diet on the kidneys because it is believed that such a diet can accelerate the progression of kidney disease. But even there are no long-term results.

8. Where does the low carb diet come from?

In the 1970s, the "low-carb" trend from the US swept across the ocean to Germany. The nutritionist Robert Atkins put his work "Dr. Atkins' Diet Revolution" new and was subsequently author of at least 17 diet counselors. Because of this countless people abstain from carbohydrates these days.

But the first to demand a low carbohydrate diet was William Osler - often dubbed the father of modern medicine. He recommended in the late 18th century overweight women to eat little starch and sugar.

Barely a century later, William Banting became known for publishing the book "Open Letter on Obesity to the Entire Audience" . In it, he advises a meat-heavy diet, paired with seven units of alcohol a day. This diet is considered the predecessor of today's Atkins diet.

9. Do you really get bad breath on a low carb diet?

In ketogenesis, three types of ketone bodies are formed: acetoacetate, 3-hydroxybutyrate and acetone. First of all, acetoacetate is formed. If too much of it is produced, acetone develops. This will give off the breath - that can then "smell". Acetone is occasionally also perceptible in diabetics as bad breath. The other two ketone body types are excreted in the urine. With a test strip can be tested by a proof of the ketone body, if you are really in the ketogenesis.

10. Does the feeling of hunger during a low carb diet decrease?

The increased ketone body concentration seems to provide according to some studies for a stronger feeling of satiety in the willing to lose weight. However, experimental evidence for this hypothesis is still pending. Another benefit of a high-protein diet might be that the release of the hormone glucagon is promoted. The glucagon in turn suppresses another hormone called ghrelin. This is a growth hormone that normally acts appetizing. In theory, less ghrelin is also less hungry. However, since the feeling of hunger is always individual, it is also possible to make only limited scientific statements.

Summary

According to Dr. Kabat , in the last century we have become more vulnerable to lack of attention . We're going so fast and we're so worried that without realizing it, our neurological abilities are changing. The lifestyle increasingly promotes isolation. In this last century we have moved away from nature and life in society and this has accelerated with the digital revolution. These tools were designed to "save time" but instead, there are now more things to attend to and it is more difficult to pay attention to just one thing.....

So how can MINDFULNESS help us?

Mindfulness is a term that means “FULL ATTENTION” and its origin dates back to Buddhist psychology for more than 25 centuries. This concept arises from the hand of Dr

Kabat Zinn , doctor and founder of the Stress Reduction Clinic at the University of Massachusetts in 1979.

This method he called Mindfulness Based Stress Reduction (MBSR) tested it through scientific variables in thousands of patients. He measured values within the brain and medical parameters, experiencing improvements in all of them. Then he began to spread the benefits of this practice away from religious and spiritual connotations. It did not take long to admit Mindfulness as a tool of profound benefits in the field of health until science ended up integrating it as a useful and effective tool.

From a scientific perspective, there is a consensus in defining mindfulness as a mental function that allows us to keep the focus of attention on a present experience. The brain is like a plastic and is constantly changing. Habits like Mindfulness vary communication between neurons and modify certain neuronal structures. Their practice seems to increase the capacity for attention, concentration and learning. It also improves the memory and immune system of individuals. In addition, his practice calms and develops empathy with others.

Through exercises, techniques and learning Mindfulness tools we will improve the performance of the BRAIN OF

THE CHILD. And how is it done ?; In short, experiencing life through the information provided by THE SENSES , that is; May your thoughts be in tune with your body.

To MINDFULNESS need a place and a particular position?

No, like every habit, it is easier to acquire if you practice it with a certain routine but nothing more than your ability to concentrate is necessary. We can all do it!! You can practice at any time of the day and in any situation (even the one that causes you the most stress). MINDFULNESS will help you control the situations that scare you most.

What physical benefits are obtained with this practice?

It helps us control frustration by accepting reality

It helps us focus on what really matters

Our brain exercises and ages less

It is a stress reliever and anxiety

Our body improves its immune capacity

The ability to maintain attention is improved

Relieves chronic pain

It helps us to know ourselves and improves our SELF-CONCEPT.

There are already examples of educational centers that have launched innovation PROJECTS with the introduction of MINDFULNESS techniques. There are initiatives such as:

Happy Classrooms Program in Aragon

Treva Program in Catalonia

Conscious Schools in the Valencian Community

There are many famous and professional athletes who apply the practice of Mindfulness to improve their mental concentration and manage their emotions. Meg Ryan, Goldie Hawn and Oprah Winfrey confirmed practicing it to feel better and live more connected to themselves. The tennis player Novak Djokovic in his book "The secrets of the winner", speaks of the importance that mindfulness played in his life and in the takeoff of his sports career.

"There is an important method that I use to conserve my energy level, even when negative feelings are filtered. Psychologists call it a state of mindfulness... it is a type of meditation in which, instead of trying to silence your mind or find "inner peace," you allow and accept your thoughts as they come, objectively, without judging them, While you are aware of that moment. "

In western society they have learned to heal themselves when they are sick but have not taught them to prevent disease. When they appear, they treat them with medications that silence the pain but do not explain the cause. In some countries of Asia such as China, India or Japan, in addition to using medicine to cure, they understand that it is necessary to know and develop tools to prevent diseases and thus know their origins. Today, with the globalization and intercommunication that exists in the world.

Conclusion

There are different types of hunger. For example, you can be hungry with your eyes when you see a nice piece of brownie passing by, hungry with your mouth when you taste a bite and taste it for more, hungry with your cells craving for the right nutrients or hungry with your heart if you have heartache. It is interesting to consider this. Maybe after a single serving your body will have enough while your mouth says: give me just another piece of creamy lemon pie!

To optimally digest your food, it is important to chew long and well. This way your food is already pre-digested and mixed with digestive enzymes. If you do not do this, it will end up in too large parts of your stomach and your digestive system will not function optimally. You can then suffer from heartburn, burping, bloating and other ailments. Here you can immediately make a link with mindful food. If we take the time to empty our plates, we automatically chew more slowly.

Being mindful means being in the here and now. So observe what is currently without judgment or criticism. Before you eat you can also ask yourself: am I really hungry now? Or am I just tired, bored or seeing something delicious. By getting more in contact with your body, you feel better what you need at that moment. This is a case of practice makes perfect, but you can imagine how great the results are.

People always find it very cool to notice that if they eat something unhealthy, but enjoy it very consciously, it usually also works out well. As if the body agrees because you enjoy it so much. The opposite is when you eat half a bar of chocolate in frustration. Stomach makes strange (angry?) Noises.

Around 1900 there was one Mr. Fletcher living in San Francisco. He lost more than 20 kilos because he started to chew his food better. Quickly 'fluttering' was all the rage. Research did not only show that chewing was super good for your general health, but that chess problems could also be solved much better. People's brain function is therefore improved by enjoying meals for longer.

Sounds like there are really many benefits to mindful food. Jan Chozen Bays confirms that in her book 'mindful eating'. According to her, by eating more consciously and slower you can taste much more. More chewing means that more different flavors are released. Nutrients are also much better broken down because they are already mixed with the enzymes from our saliva. That means that your body gets more nutrition from eating less. Sounds good right? Another advantage is that you can feel better when you are full. This signal only arrives in your brain after 20 minutes.

The question: how are you going to do this? How can you ensure that you eat your food with a lot of attention? We all have a lot of things to do in a day and food is often something that happens just as quickly in between. Fletcher would say that you have to chew each bite at least 32 times. I strongly support the principle: step by step. For example, you can start chewing this 32 times only with the first bites and you may find that it will eventually happen on its own. Things that I use to eat more mindfully are consciously looking at my plate, showing gratitude for my food and not doing other things while eating. So the computer closes and I put my book far away. Sometimes difficult when I eat alone, but it is worth it!

To return to the question I mentioned in the first paragraph. What if you eat very healthy but not mindful? I don't believe in one solution. I think that everything we do in our lives contributes to how healthy and happy we feel. Yet I put mindful food higher on the list than healthy food. If you are mindful you enjoy more, you value more and you make better choices. After all, you are much more in contact with what those choices have for your body and mind. You therefore automatically choose food faster which gives you energy and strength.

Do you eat mindful? Is it easy for you to eat consciously or do you have difficulty with it? I am very curious about your reactions!

Lightning Source UK Ltd.
Milton Keynes UK
UKHW022218051120
372880UK00003B/253

9 781914 039454